# A THEORY OF UNIVERSALS
## *Universals and Scientific Realism*
### VOLUME II

T0370904

# A Theory
# of Universals

UNIVERSALS AND SCIENTIFIC REALISM
VOLUME II

## D. M. Armstrong

*Challis Professor of Philosophy, University of Sydney*

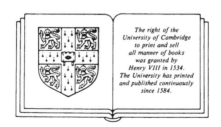

The right of the
University of Cambridge
to print and sell
all manner of books
was granted by
Henry VIII in 1534.
The University has printed
and published continuously
since 1584.

*Cambridge University Press*

CAMBRIDGE

NEW YORK   PORT CHESTER

MELBOURNE   SYDNEY

CAMBRIDGE UNIVERSITY PRESS
Cambridge, New York, Melbourne, Madrid, Cape Town, Singapore, São Paulo, Delhi

Cambridge University Press
The Edinburgh Building, Cambridge CB2 8RU, UK

Published in the United States of America by Cambridge University Press, New York

www.cambridge.org
Information on this title: www.cambridge.org/9780521280327

First published 1978
First paperback edition 1980
Reprinted 1990
Re-issued in this digitally printed version 2009

A catalogue record for this publication is available from the British Library

ISBN 978-0-521-21950-1 hardback
ISBN 978-0-521-28032-7 paperback

# Contents

## Volume II: A Theory of Universals

# The argument of Volume I

It should be possible to read *A Theory of Universals* without having read its predecessor, *Nominalism and Realism*. A brief recapitulation of the argument of volume I is, however, essential.

An introductory Part considers the notion of a *predicate*. In contemporary fashion, predicates are taken to be certain linguistic expressions which are parts of sentences. Under what conditions should we say that different predicate-tokens are tokens of the same predicate-type? For the most part, phonetic–orthographic criteria are inconvenient for philosophical purposes. So it is laid down that such tokens are instances of the same type if and only if they are synonymous. A convention is introduced. Where phonetic–orthographic identity-conditions are intended, the predicate is supplied with double quotation-marks. Where, as is usual, semantic identity-conditions are intended, the predicate is given single quotation-marks only.

The second Part of volume I is an extended critique of Nominalism, together with Platonic, that is, Transcendent Realism. Nominalism is defined as the doctrine that everything there is is a particular and nothing but a particular. A Realist is one who denies this proposition, holding that universals exist.

It is argued that in the dispute between Nominalism and Realism the onus of proof lies with the Nominalist. For the distinction between token and type is apparently all-pervasive and *prima facie* incompatible with Nominalism. Five Nominalist strategies for analysing the proposition that an object, *a*, has a property, F, are distinguished:

> *Predicate Nominalism:* a has the property, F, if and only if a falls under the predicate 'F'
> *Concept Nominalism:* a has the property, F, if and only if a falls under the concept F
> *Class Nominalism:* a has the property, F, if and only if a is a member of the class of Fs

*Mereological Nominalism:* a has the property, F, if and only if a is part of the aggregate (heap) of the Fs

*Resemblance Nominalism:* a has the property, F, if and only if a suitably resembles the paradigm case(s) of an F.

These analyses are criticized in detail in successive chapters. One simple line of criticism, among the many which are brought, is that in each analysis the particular, *a*, has the property, F, in virtue of its *relation* to something external to it: predicate, concept, class, aggregate or paradigm. Yet it is intuitively clear that *a* might be F even if none of these things existed. Transcendent Realism is equally a Relational analysis:

a has the property, F, if and only if a "participates" in the transcendent Form, F

and the same criticism can be brought against it.

Besides these criticisms of Nominalism, a short chapter recapitulates arguments used by Arthur Pap, and recently strengthened by Frank Jackson, to show that the truth of certain statements demands the existence of universals. Examples are:

(1) Red(ness) resembles orange(ness) more than it resembles blue(ness)

and

(2) Red(ness) is a colour.

Pap's argument for the necessity of attribute variables ('He has the same virtues as his father') is also briefly rehearsed.

The second Part of volume I ends with a chapter on Particularism, the doctrine, associated with G. F. Stout and many others, that properties and relations of particulars are not universals but are, like the things which have the properties and relations, particulars. It is contended, first, that the arguments for Particularism are inconclusive; second, that Particularism leaves the Problem of Universals unsolved, a problem which can only be solved by admitting universal properties and relations over and above the Particularist's properties and relations; third, that once this admission has been made, no coherent account can be given of the relation between particular properties (and relations) and the corresponding universal properties (and relations).

The third Part of volume I begins by asking whether, since it seems that we are forced to postulate universals in any case, we should follow Russell and others in giving an account of particulars as nothing but "bundles of universals". Various reasons, including a traditional line of argument based upon the Identity of Indiscernibles, are given for rejecting this view. It is concluded that, just as the Nominalist errs in trying to reduce universals to particulars, so this Universalist view errs in trying to reduce particulars to universals.

The question then arises how the irreducible particularity of particulars stands to their irreducible universality (their properties and relations). With Transcendent Realism rejected, some form of Immanent Realism must be accepted. A thing's properties must be brought within the thing. *Relational* Immanent Realism takes the particularity of a particular to be a substratum standing in an indescribable relation to its properties. An argument, in effect F. H. Bradley's regress, is advanced against this view.

It is concluded, therefore, that although particularity and universality are inseparable aspects of all existence, they are neither reducible to each other nor are they related. Though distinct, their union is closer than relation. Scotus talked of a mere "formal distinction" between the thisness and the nature of particulars. The situation is admittedly profoundly puzzling, but, it is suggested, the Scotist view is the most satisfactory one which can be found. A comparison which may be useful is the way in which shape and size are united in a particular.

A *state of affairs* is then defined as a particular's having a property, or two or more particulars' being related by a relation. We may consider particulars along with their properties, or else in abstraction from all their properties. This yields two conceptions of a particular. It is the latter conception which is involved in the conception of a state of affairs. For the former, or "thick", conception already is the conception of a state of affairs. It seems, therefore, that we can say both that the world is a world of particulars (in the "thick" sense) and that it is a world of states of affairs.

Some universals already involve the notion of a state of affairs. These are the "particularizing" universals, of which *being a man* would be an instance in the unlikely event that the predicate 'a man' applies in virtue of something genuinely common to all men. Such universals divide their instances into non-overlapping individuals (individual men). A universal of this sort may be said to particularize *strongly*. *Being one kilogram of lead*, however, is only a *weakly* particularizing universal (if it is a universal at all) because its instances overlap. The necessity for the notion of a particularizing universal emerges most clearly when it is noted that *being two men* and *being two kilograms of lead* have equal claims with the two previous examples to be universals. These new universals involve the notion of being made up of two *instances* of the original universals. That is, they already involve the notion of a state of affairs.

If we take a particular four-dimensionally ("as a space-time worm"), then it may be said to occupy a certain spatio-temporal position. The question arises whether this "total" position can be identified with the particularity of a particular. Since it is logically possible that there are particulars which are not spatio-temporal, the concepts of particularity and total position cannot be identical. But if everything there is is spatio-temporal, as it is plausible to assert, particularity may *in fact* be identical with total position. We thus reach the view that it is a particular's total position plus its properties (including its spatio-temporal *properties*) which constitute a particular in the "thick" sense.

There is reason to think that more than one particular can occupy the very same total position. Possible examples are the "visual cube" and the "tactual cube". The particular constituted by the sum of all the particulars at a certain total position may be called a *concrete* particular. Its "parts" may be called '*abstract*' particulars. It appears, then, that different particulars may have the same particularity, *viz*. the same total position. They must then have different properties. Contrariwise, different particulars may have the very same properties. They must then have different total position. But a certain total position plus a certain set of properties yields an unrepeatable particular ("a substance").

In the last chapter of volume I a world-hypothesis is advanced. The hypothesis is that the world consists of nothing but particulars having properties and relations (monadic and polyadic universals). It is argued in the last Part of volume II that these universals themselves have certain properties and relations (the relations constituting the *laws of nature*). But with this exception, it is suggested, no other sorts of entity need be recognized. This hypothesis is less economical than the Nominalist world-hypothesis: that the world contains nothing but particulars. But it is still economical. It involves rejecting transcendent universals, realms of numbers, transcendent values, timeless propositions, non-existent objects ("the golden mountain"), *possibilia*, possible worlds and "abstract" classes.

A general argument is given against postulating any of these entities. They all lack *causal* power: they do not act. It is then argued that we have no good reason to postulate anything which has no effect upon the spatio-temporal world.

It is not argued that statements about numbers, propositions, possibilities, classes, etc. are false. But it is suggested that it should be possible to give an account of the truth-conditions of the statements purely in terms of particulars, their properties and their relations. No detailed account of the truth-conditions is given. All that is proposed is a *research-programme*, one that is obviously too vast to be carried out in this work. The argument from lack of causal power is simply intended as a reason for thinking that the research-programme is a promising one.

# 13

# *Relations between predicates and universals*

## 1 *Empiricism and universals*

We may begin this volume by noticing a complaint against any theory of objective universals made by David Pears in a well-known article (1951). He says that the believer in universals is tempted to "explain" the use of the same predicate to apply to different particulars by giving an obviously circular formula: "We are able to call things red because they are red" (p. 38). Alan Donagan (1963) criticizes Pears, pointing out that he fails to note the shift from mention to use of the predicate 'red' in the course of the sentence (p. 151). "We are able to call things 'red' because they are red", is not circular at all. Donagan is, of course, formally correct.

Nevertheless, there is something which looks too good to be true about the amended formula. A predicate, a man-made thing, is applied to certain particulars and is applicable to an indefinite number of further particulars. It is then assumed by many Realists that we are automatically entitled to conclude that an objective property, or, in the case of many-place predicates, an objective relation, corresponds to the predicate. But no philosopher with any Empiricist sympathies can feel happy with a conclusion so easily reached. There seems to be no honest toil in it! Here, I believe, we come upon a deep reason why Empiricists have been attracted to one or another variety of Nominalism: because to accept Realism seemed to commit them to objective properties and relations wherever there was a corresponding predicate. *The rejection of Realism about universals was part of the Empiricist rejection of the notion that one can establish the existence of entities by a priori reasoning.*[1]

I share the Empiricist prejudices on method, but at the same time I find no version of Nominalism satisfactory. I am thus led to consider a purged Realism. I suggest that we reject the notion that just because the predicate 'red' applies to an open class of particulars, therefore there must be a property, *redness*. There must be an explanation why the predicate is applicable to an indefinite class of particulars which played no part in our learning the meaning of the word "red". Furthermore, this explanation must in the end appeal to the *properties* (or relations) of these particulars. But none of this shows that there is a property, *redness*.

What properties and relations there are in the world is to be decided by total science, that is, the sum total of all enquiries into the nature of things. (Philosophy is part of total science, but a mere part and not the most important part.) The question is not to be determined simply by consulting our predicates, although we must begin from, and must not despise, the clues to what properties and relations there are which our predicates offer us.

Philosophers are familiar with the idea that science attempts to discover the laws of nature. Laws of nature link particulars falling under certain universals with the same or different particulars falling under certain other universals, in more or less complex patterns. Further, philosophers are familiar with the idea that it is a weariness and a labour to establish in any degree what these law-like patterns are. But philosophers have tended to assume that there is no particular difficulty in identifying the universals themselves. For many Realists, predicates automatically pick out objective universals. (For Nominalists, or Predicate Nominalists at least, predicates also pick

---

[1] In volume I, we have already met two other reasons which may help to explain the appeal of Nominalism. The first was encountered in ch. 1 § 1. As Strawson notes, predicates have a fixed number of gaps where referring expressions must be inserted if a sentence is to result. Referring expressions themselves, however, may be inserted in the gaps quite promiscuously. Since universals are correlated with predicates, particulars with referring expressions, the impression is given that universals are dependent beings, particulars independent. The second reason is the phenomenon of the "victory of particularity" to which attention was drawn in ch. 11 § III. The particularity or thisness of a particular plus its properties (which are universals) yields *not* a universal but a *particular*. (This is the "thick" conception of a particular.) Hence it is easy, though wrong, to think that the world consists of particulars to the exclusion of universals.

out universals, because "universals" are simply shadows cast by the predicates.)

What has to be realized, instead, is that determining what universals there are is as much a matter for laborious enquiry as determining how universals are linked in laws. (The two enterprises are, of course, bound up with each other.) Philosophy may have some part to play in the enquiry into what universals there are, but it would be presumptuous folly to think that it has a major role.

The position I wish to reject may be formulated in an admittedly extremist fashion: predicates stand in a one–one correlation to universals. By "predicates" here is meant, of course, predicate-*types*. For each predicate-type, there exists its own peculiar universal. For each universal, there exists its own peculiar predicate. Perhaps there are no philosophers who would actually hold both these propositions, particularly after a few "reminders" have been assembled. But many philosophers reason *as if* they accepted these propositions. This is the model which dominates their thought. In any case, the propositions will serve as a useful limiting case by contrast with which I can advance a completely different view.

The correct view I take to be this. Given a predicate, there may be none, one or many universals in virtue of which the predicate applies. Given a universal, there may be none, one or many predicates which apply in virtue of that universal. In the remainder of this chapter, the two cases of predicates to which no universal corresponds and universals to which no predicate corresponds will be considered. The difficult, and ground-breaking, cases are those which involve one predicate but many universals, and, again, many predicates but only one universal. They will be considered in the later chapters of this Part.

## II *Predicates without universals*

All properties and relations are the properties and relations of particulars. By the Principle of Instantiation, for all properties, P, there exists a particular, $x$, such that $x$ is P. For all relations, R, there exist particulars, $x, y$ . . . such that Rxy . . . "Exists" here must not be construed as "exists *now*". The existential quantifier has nothing to do with the present moment. That $(\exists x)(\text{Dodo } x)$ is *true*, although, presumably, that $(\exists x)(\text{Unicorn } x)$ is false. A universal exists if there was, is or will be particulars having that property or standing in that relation.

There are predicates which apply to no particular, past, present or future. The predicate 'accelerates through the speed of light' *may* be such a predicate. But if nothing past, present or future accelerates through the speed of light, then there is no property of accelerating through the speed of light. No property would then correspond to this predicate. The fact that it is logically possible that something should accelerate through the speed of light does not entail that accelerating through the speed of light is a property. For a merely possible property is not a property.

Here, however, we may be reminded that there are other sorts of possibility besides logical possibility. Suppose that it is empirically possible to produce a certain heavy element, not found in nature, which, if produced, can be predicted to have a property which no other substance possesses. Suppose, however, that this element is never manufactured, perhaps because of the enormous expense. Might we not still talk about this element *and its property*?

I agree that we might well talk in this way, but I suggest that we should not take such talk seriously for the purpose of ontology. We also speak of particulars in the same way. For instance, we may speak of "the walk we never took that day". The walk is not a particular alongside the walks which do get taken, nor are we inclined to think it is. If mere empirical possibility endows properties with existence, then why does it not do the same for particulars? Why not admit the present King of France as a particular? It is empirically possible that France be a monarchy.

This is not to say that predicates to which no property corresponds may not have their value in the classification of actual things. It is often convenient to classify things in terms of their degree of approximation to "ideal cases" which do not, or even cannot, exist. But a useful fiction is still a fiction.

In the cases considered so far in this section, there is no particular to which the predicate applies. *A fortiori*, therefore, there is no universal in virtue of which the predicate applies. But there seem to be other predicates which do have application to particulars but which fail to apply in virtue of some universal. Every particular is identical with itself. So the predicate 'identical with itself' applies to each particular. But we are not thereby forced to admit that particulars have a property, *being identical with themselves*.

Two reasons may be given for denying that there is any such property. First, we know *a priori* that a thing must be identical with itself. Now if we take seriously the idea that what properties there are is a matter for scientific investigation, then the existence of this *a priori* knowledge is a good reason for denying that *being identical with itself* is a property. The principle of method involved is one to which constant appeal will be made in this work. It may be formulated in Irish fashion: if it can be proved *a priori* that a thing falls under a certain universal, then there is no such universal.

Second, we may appeal to a plausible necessary condition for something's being a property. If a particular has a property, that property must endow the particular with some specific causal power, or if the property is causally idle, then it must at least be an intelligible hypothesis that the property should endow particulars with some specific causal power. (It would seem, however, that we could never have any good reason to postulate the existence of causally idle properties. Such properties would never make their presence felt in any way, and so would be undetectable.) Now could a thing's identity with itself even be conceived to endow the object with causal power? It is difficult to see how it could. This is another principle to which constant appeal will be made in this work.

The same two considerations appear to show that 'exists' is a predicate to which no property (or relation) corresponds.

Why is it that philosophers have thought, or have been tempted to think, that to each distinct predicate-type there corresponds its own peculiar universal? I think that the answer is clear. It is the influence of the Argument from Meaning which has so often, and so fatally, distorted the Problem of Universals. If universals are conceived of as meanings, and if a semantic criterion is accepted for the identity of predicates, then it follows at once that each predicate-type is associated with its own universal. Realists have then put an inflationary, Nominalists a deflationary, interpretation on this situation.

Many passages might be cited. I select the following one from the (otherwise!) excellent discussion of universals in Timothy Sprigge's *Facts, Words and Beliefs* (1970):

> I would support the doctrine of *universalia ante rem* as against the doctrine of *universalia in rebus* in the claim that to say that there is a universal of a certain kind does not imply that that universal is

exemplified. My reasons for doing so should be clear if I point out that there is a property named by 'Being a King of France in 1960' and even 'Being a round square' and that if there were not 'there is no king of France in 1960' and 'there are no round squares' *would both lack meaning* [my italics]. (p. 85 n. 1)

Yet this passage comes from an author who had earlier in this book and with much more insight written:

Do not let it be thought, however, that I postulate *redness* in order to explain the meaning of 'red'. (p. 56)

What we must do, I submit, is to distinguish with all possible sharpness between the meaning, intension, or connotation of a predicate on the one hand, and the property or relation, if there is one, in virtue of which the predicate applies to particulars, if it does apply to any, on the other. *The study of the semantics of predicates must be distinguished from the theory of universals.* Ontology and semantics must be separated – to their mutual benefit. Of course, this lays on us an obligation to give an account of the semantics of predicates. What is it for a predicate like 'accelerates through the speed of light' to be a meaningful expression? In this work, however, that problem can receive only incidental attention. Our concern here is with first philosophy. (I believe that Locke's theory of Simple and Complex Ideas gives us the clue to the solution of the problem.)

At any rate, my contention is that the case for objective universals does not rest upon the theory of meaning but upon the apparent identity of nature which is exhibited by certain particulars. This apparent identity Nominalists are unable to explain away. The argument may be presented in terms of predicates, when we ask how it is possible that the same predicate can apply to these different particulars, and conclude that it must be in virtue of the properties and/or relations which these particulars have. But, as I have already emphasized *ad nauseam* in the previous volume, the fundamental observation is an ontological one: that different particulars may nevertheless be identical in some respect.

### III  *Universals without predicates*

A Realist theory of universals must allow that there can be universals to which no predicate corresponds. A Realist theory of *perception* maintains (a) that it is an intelligible conception that physical objects should exist in independence of their being perceived; (b) that there are overwhelming, although not logically conclusive, reasons for thinking that there are such objects. Similarly, a Realist theory of universals maintains that (a) it is an intelligible conception that there are properties and relations of particulars which exist in the absence of any corresponding predicates or classifying concepts; (b) that there are overwhelming, although not logically conclusive, reasons for thinking that there are such properties and relations.

Just as we cannot perceive an unperceived object, so we cannot give an example of a universal to which no predicate corresponds. But given an object which is never perceived, it is nevertheless always intelligible that it should have been perceived. Similarly, given a universal to which no predicate corresponds, it is nevertheless always intelligible that there should have been such a predicate.

There is no upper limit to the number of universals which there could be. I have heard it maintained (by J. J. C. Smart in conversation) that the number of universals could not be greater than the number of the natural numbers, that is, the least transfinite cardinal. But the argument given for his contention shows once again the baneful influence of the theory of meaning. For the premiss of Smart's argument was that the nature of language is such that the number of *predicates* cannot be greater than the number of the natural numbers. Such an argument must be taken seriously by a Nominalist about properties (at any rate, by a *Predicate* Nominalist) but the Realist may ignore it. Why should not the number of properties exceed the number of possible predicates? Why must the limits of language be the measure of reality? It will remain true that for each property, taken individually, it is logically possible that there should be a predicate associated with that property. I may add that if it is true, as it seems to be true, that there is continuous quantity in nature, then we are forced to admit continuum-many properties. (Support for this conclusion is provided in ch. 22 § 1.)

This argument may even be turned round and made diagnostic of Predicate Nominalism. If a philosopher maintains that there cannot be more properties than the number of the natural numbers, on the ground that this is the upper limit to the number of predicates, then he shows that, whether or not he has realized it, he has embraced Predicate Nominalism.

It should be noted further that I make one assumption here which I believe to be true but which I do not know how to defend in any depth. This is the assumption that infinity in nature (as opposed to infinity in mathematics) is a genuine logical possibility. I maintain, for instance, that it is a meaningful possibility that the number of stars is the number of the natural numbers or that there are continuum-many properties. But it seems to me that the onus of proof is upon those who deny that these are genuine (logical) possibilities. It is they who, in *a priori* fashion, seek to set a limit to the nature of things, and deny that these *prima facie* logical possibilities are real logical possibilities. They may be able to make their case good by argument, but I think it is up to them to find such an argument. I do not know of any.

So, I maintain, the question whether there are or are not infinities in nature should be treated as an *a posteriori* matter, a matter into which the philosopher has no especial insight. In general, a good philosophical methodology for an Empiricist seems to be this: be rather hospitable to claims about logical possibility, reserve one's scepticism for claims about what actually exists. However, I do not wish to carry this methodology to its Quinean limit where the category of logical impossibility is denied.

Subsequent chapters will attempt to develop further the theory of universals. But at the centre of all our reasonings will lie the contention that the ways predicates and universals stand to each other differ from case to case and that it is a question for total science, not a question to be settled *a priori*, what universals there are.

## IV *Types of predicate*

But before going any further it will be convenient to make a classification of predicates.

We may distinguish first between "open" predicates and predicates which are "closed". The essential mark of an open predicate is that there is nothing in its *semantics* which restricts its application to a finite number of particulars. It may as a matter of fact apply only to one, or only to a finite number, of particulars. But this will be a matter of fact, not of meaning. If a predicate is not open, it is "closed". 'Identical with the planet Venus' and 'the wisest of men' are closed predicates. The notions of open and closed predicates are substitutes for the traditional notions, already referred to in volume I, of "open" and "closed" classes. The distinction cannot be drawn at the level of classes without reference to the class-predicate or concept. So it seems convenient to draw the distinction at the level of predicates from the very beginning.

Predicates may be divided further into predicates which are "pure" and those which are "impure" (see Loux, 1974). The predicate 'descended from Charlemagne' is an open predicate. There is nothing in the semantics of the predicate which prevents it applying to an infinite number of particulars. Charlemagne's line may never fail. But the predicate is impure, because it involves essential reference to a particular: Charlemagne. 'Descended from kings', on the other hand, is a pure predicate, involving as it does no essential reference to any particular.

Since 'descended from Charlemagne' makes essential reference to a particular, *being descended from Charlemagne* cannot even be a *prima facie* case of a universal. We thus see the inadequacy of Aristotle's famous definition of the term:

> By the term 'universal' I mean that which is of such a nature as to be predicated of many subjects, by 'individual' that which is not thus predicated. (17a, 37–40)

For *being descended from Charlemagne* would appear to fit this definition of "universal". Aristotle has given a necessary but not a sufficient condition for being a universal. Indeed, unless "predicated" is read as "capable of being predicated" it will not even be necessary.

The definition does, however, exclude *being the wisest of men* from being a universal. This is as it should be, because 'the wisest of men', although a pure predicate, is not an open predicate.

From the standpoint of the theory of universals it is, of course, predicates which are both pure and open which are of especial interest. I propose to divide such predicates into no less than five sub-classes. It will be seen that the five classes represent different degrees on a single scale.

(1) First there are *strictly universal* predicates. These are predicates which apply in virtue of a single universal alone, monadic or polyadic, a property or a relation. (Single need not mean simple.) Since it is an *a posteriori* question, to be decided by total science, what universals there are, no uncontroversial example of a strictly

universal predicate can be given. A reasonably plausible example is 'weighs one kilogram exactly'.

Strictly universal predicates may be sub-divided into "property-predicates" and "relation-predicates".

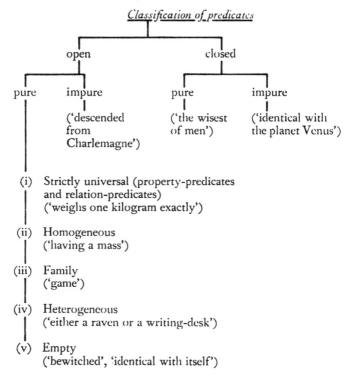

*Classification of predicates*

open      closed

pure    impure      pure    impure

('descended from Charlemagne')    ('the wisest of men')    ('identical with the planet Venus')

(i)   Strictly universal (property-predicates and relation-predicates) ('weighs one kilogram exactly')

(ii)   Homogeneous ('having a mass')

(iii)   Family ('game')

(iv)   Heterogeneous ('either a raven or a writing-desk')

(v)   Empty ('bewitched', 'identical with itself')

Fig. 1

Strictly universal predicates are very important for our purposes, especially in this Part. Oddly enough, however, they are not very important in theoretical science. This is because, as a matter of scientific fact, law-like connection in nature does not normally take the form of a connection between single universals, but rather between *classes* of universals (see ch. 22 § v).

(2) This brings us to the second type of pure, open, predicate which will be called a *homogeneous* predicate. Such predicates do not apply in virtue of a single universal, but rather in virtue of some member of a whole class of distinct universals. But for the predicate

to be homogeneous, the class must have a definite formal structure. The universals must be held together by a unitary general formula of a purely formal, that is, topic-neutral sort. It is classes of universals thus unified, so we find, which are linked by laws of nature.

For the present, I leave the characterization of the classes of universals involved rather vague. It will not be possible to be more precise until ch. 22. In the meantime, I simply give as (plausible) examples the classes of all the (different) lengths, masses and temperatures.

(3) The third class of predicates that are both pure and open will be called *family* predicates. The predicate 'game' may well be an example. A family predicate again applies in virtue of some member of a class of universals. But the class, although having a degree of unity, lacks that unitary formal structure to be found in the classes associated with homogeneous predicates. Such predicates may be used in science, but they are used *faute de mieux*.

(4) It should now be clear that our successive types of predicate represent successive fallings away from the limiting or ideal case of *identity* of universal in virtue of which "strictly universal" predicates apply. After family predicates, then, come *heterogeneous* predicates. Such predicates apply in virtue of some member of a class of universals, but the class does not even have a 'family' unity. The disjunctive predicate 'either a raven or a writing-desk' would be an example. (It will be argued in the next chapter that there are no disjunctive universals.)

(5) Finally, there are what may be called *empty* predicates. These are predicates which either have no application, or, if they do apply, do not apply in virtue of universals at all. An example of the first sort of predicate is 'bewitched', of the second 'identical with itself'.

It should be noted that even impure predicates will, in general, apply in virtue of universals. For the predicate 'descended from Charlemagne' to apply to a particular, the particular must have certain properties and relations. But the particular must also be related to another particular: Charlemagne himself.

In conclusion, a word must be added about properties and relations. We could instead speak of monadic and polyadic universals. (Properties are monadic universals. It will be argued in ch. 18 § 1 and ch. 19 § VI, that all monadic universals are properties.) Now if we take seriously the notion that particulars can only have the same property or the same relation if they are *identical* to each other in some respect, then some revision of ordinary discourse will be necessary. We shall have to accept that what ordinary discourse refers to as properties and relations are often not properties and relations in the sense in which the terms are used in this book.

Am I simply, then, re-defining the terms "property" and "relation" and so involving myself in all the intellectual disadvantages which contemporary philosophy has shown to flow from such re-definitions? Would it be better to speak only of monadic and polyadic universals? I think not. For what I call properties and relations may fairly be claimed to be the *real* properties and relations. It is in terms of them that an account of the nature of the world is to be given. The properties and relations of ordinary discourse which are neither identical with, nor firmly linked with, monadic and polyadic universals are mere creatures of discourse. It is true of them, as the Predicate Nominalist would claim of *all* properties and relations, that they are mere shadows cast on the world by our predicates. We are therefore, I think, entitled to use the old and honourable terms "property" and "relation" in a way which will do better justice to the structure of being. At any rate, for good or ill, I serve notice that this is the way in which the terms are used officially in this work. The looser, popular, usage will be convenient occasionally, especially in the case of the term "relation". It should not cause confusion.

We can now go on to consider certain pure predicates with the object of showing that they are not strictly universal predicates.

# 14

# *Rejection of disjunctive and negative universals*

Let it be given that 'P', 'Q' ... etc. are all strictly universal predicates (property-predicates or relation-predicates), applying in virtue of distinct universals. What is the status of predicates which are formed from these strictly universal predicates solely by means of truth-functional connectives? They are certainly predicates that are open and pure. Are they strictly universal predicates? In particular, do the predicates 'PVQ', '~P' and 'P&Q' apply to the objects to which they apply solely in virtue of a single universal? In other words, are there disjunctive, negative and conjunctive universals? This chapter will be devoted to arguing that there are no disjunctive or negative universals. The next chapter will maintain that there are conjunctive universals. The enquiry, and the results arrived at, will take us quite deep into the theory of universals.

Let it be re-emphasized that there are no merely syntactical tests for strictly universal predicates. It is perfectly possible that predicates having the *linguistic* form 'FVG' or '~H' should turn out to be property-predicates. The mark of a universal, that is to say, a property or a relation, is that it is genuinely identical in different particulars. And whether or not we have genuine identity is to be decided, so far as it can be decided, by examining not language but the world. So it will simply be assumed in the course of the next two chapters that we have been able to identify certain universals and, therefore, certain strictly universal predicates. The legitimate question how exactly scientific enquiry achieves, or attempts to achieve, these identifications will be left until ch. 16.

## 1 *Rejection of disjunctive universals*

I begin by advancing three arguments against the existence of disjunctive properties. They are not conclusive, but they appear to be weighty. The theory which will be criticized is that *any* predicate of the form 'PVQ', where 'P' and 'Q' are property-predicates, is itself a (disjunctive) property-predicate. I concede that it might be possible to develop a less wholesale theory of disjunctive properties which might evade some (but not I think all) of these arguments. The same sort of arguments can be brought against disjunctive relations. It is, of course, "classical" disjunction, governed by the ordinary truth-table rules, which we are considering. In ch. 22 § 1, brief mention will be made of the possibility that science may have to admit non-classical disjunctive properties, for instance in order to explain quantum phenomena.

First, disjunctive properties offend against the principle that a genuine property is identical in its different particulars. Suppose *a* has a property P but lacks Q, while *b* has Q but lacks P. It seems laughable to conclude from these premisses that *a* and *b* are identical in some respect. Yet both have the "property", *P or Q*.

Second, if *a* is P, then an indefinite number of distinct predicates of the form 'PV—' will apply to *a*, where another property-predicate is substituted for the blank. Hence we can know *a priori* that the particular, *a*, will have an indefinite number of disjunctive properties: at least as many as there are properties. But an *a priori* proof that an object has certain properties should be taken as an argument for saying that it has not got those properties. For what, and how many, properties a thing has is not to be determined *a priori*.

Third, the postulation of disjunctive properties breaks the link which it is natural to make between the properties of things and the causal powers of things. Suppose, again, that *a* has P but lacks Q. The predicate 'PVQ' applies to *a*. Nevertheless, when *a* acts, it will surely act only in virtue of its being P. Its *being P or Q* will add no power to its arm. This suggests that *being P or Q* is not a property.

Having given reasons for not admitting disjunctive properties, it is now necessary to develop a semantic theory which enables us to see how disjunctive predicates can be applicable, but not applicable in virtue of disjunctive properties.

Let P be a property, and let *a* be P. Consider now the proposition that *a* is P. It is propositions which are said to be true or false, and so, on the traditional version of the correspondence theory of truth, this proposition is said to correspond to reality. Supporters of this traditional view have then been faced with an awkward choice. They can hypostatize propositions, which makes it easy to understand the *correspondence*, but constitutes an embarrassing addition to their ontology. Alternatively they can try to give an analysis of talk about propositions without asserting that there are such objects, leaving it uncertain what "correspondence" can mean. In my opinion, the traditional correspondence theory cannot resolve this dilemma satisfactorily.

I suggest, however, that we consider not the proposition but instead the vehicle for the expression of this proposition: the *sentence* 'Pa'. There is a correspondence between this sentence and the world when this sentence "expresses a true proposition" and a failure of correspondence when it "expresses a false proposition". (Single quotes have been used for the dummy sentence to indicate that the criterion of identity adopted for the sentence-type 'Pa' is synonymy. It is, of course, sentence-types, not tokens, with which we are concerned here. See the discussion of identity-conditions for predicates in ch. 1 § II.) The comparison of a sentence to a map is helpful here. It is maps (sentences) which correspond or fail to correspond to the reality which they map, not the proposition which the map (sentence) "asserts".

These correspondences and failures of correspondence of sentences to the world are, of course, *semantic* relations or lack of relations. (Using "relation" in its popular sense here, a sense which commits us to nothing more than the applicability of a many-place predicate.) There is much which philosophers still do not understand about such relations, and so much which we cannot explicate here. But it does seem clear that there must be such correspondences and failures of correspondence between sentence-types and the world.

Now in the case of the dummy sentence-type 'Pa', which expresses the true proposition that *a* has the property P, the correspondence is of a particularly simple sort. We can think of the sentence-type as an ordered pair of expression-types < 'a', 'P' >. It is a necessary but not sufficient condition for correspondence that 'a' should have a correspondent, *a*; and that 'P' should have a correspondent, P. (Remember that just as there are referring expressions which fail of actual reference, so there are predicates to which no universal or universals correspond.) Given this condition, 'Pa' corresponds if and only if the object *a* has the property P. *a*'s having P is a *state of affairs* (for states of affairs, see ch. 11 § III).

This correspondence between the sentence 'Pa' and the world is of a very simple sort: one sentence-type, one (token) state of affairs as a correspondent, and a simple correspondence-rule. (We can call the correspondent the "truth-maker" for 'Pa' provided we remember that our ordinary notions of truth and falsity attach to propositions not sentences.) Now the great, if unconscious, error of the Correspondence theory of truth, a far more serious error than that of attributing the correspondence to propositions rather than sentences, has lain in assuming that this simple type of correspondence or lack of correspondence holds for every sort of sentence. Deliverance from this error we owe, of course, to Wittgenstein and Russell in the *Tractatus* and *The Philosophy of Logical Atomism* respectively.

Consider, in particular, the dummy sentence '(PVQ)a', where 'P' and 'Q' are property-predicates and the sentence "expresses a true proposition". (For the moment, I write '(PVQ)a' instead of the logicians' 'Pa V Qa'.) Given that the same simple correspondence-rule holds for 'Pa' then we would be *forced* to postulate a disjunctive property, *being P or Q*. (Similarly, given the truth of what is expressed by ' ~ Pa' we would be forced to postulate a negative property, *not being P*.)

In fact, however, we are not forced to postulate such a disjunctive property. We can avoid such a property by sophisticating our correspondence-rule for disjunctive predicates, a sophistication of an obvious and plausible sort. We can say that '(PVQ)a' does not correspond in the way that 'Pa' or 'Qa' corresponds. Rather, the sentence '(PVQ)a' corresponds, and so "the proposition it expresses is true", if and only if at least one of 'Pa' and 'Qa' corresponds in the original, simple, way. In other words, 'Pa v Qa' is not only the correct Russellian symbolization: it presents the situation less misleadingly than '(PVQ)a'.

"But this is just the truth-table for disjunction." It is no more than that, but familiarity with the truth-table should not be allowed to obscure the fact that the correspondence-rule used is different from the correspondence-rule used for 'Pa' and 'Qa'. Call the original correspondence "simple" correspondence. The new rule does not demand that '(PVQ)a' have simple correspondence, but instead that at least one of 'Pa' and 'Qa' have simple correspondence. This is a different type of correspondence. And once we see that it is a different type of correspondence, the need to postulate a disjunctive property to correspond to the disjunctive predicate is removed.

It may be said that this manœuvre has not "got rid of disjunction". For the correspondence-rule says that at least one *or* the other of the sentences 'Pa' or 'Qa' must correspond to the world. But this comment shows a misunderstanding of what is being claimed. No attempt is being made to give a reductive analysis of disjunctive propositions. That is not possible. All that is being claimed is that the truth of certain disjunctive propositions does not require that we postulate disjunctive properties of things. For the sentences which express these propositions can correspond to the world in a way which does not require such properties. As we may put it, in the expression 'P or Q' the word 'or' does not help to point to some feature of the world, but instead instructs us in the nature of the correspondence-rules which apply.

In concluding this section, it must be admitted that few metaphysicians have wished to postulate disjunctive universals. To that extent I have been fighting shadows. But the value of our discussion has rather been to help us see more clearly when we discuss the more difficult and controversial case of negative universals.

## II  *Rejection of negative universals*

For simplicity's sake we may once again confine ourselves to discussing the case of properties. I think that everything which is said will apply *mutatis mutandis* to relations.

The case of negative properties is more controversial than that of disjunctive properties. The hypothesis to be argued *against* may be stated thus. Given that 'P' is any property-predicate, then, if '~P' has application, it is a property-predicate also. (The demand that '~P' have application is made to satisfy the Principle of Instantiation. If everything has property P, and so nothing lacks P, the Principle alone would debar '~P' from being a property-predicate.) I begin by advancing arguments against the existence of negative properties.

First, when '~P' applies to a number of particulars, it is implausible to suggest that the predicate applies because the particulars are identical in some respect. If particulars are identical in a respect, then they resemble each other. But it is surely implausible to suggest that *not being P* is a point in which *a*, *b*, *c* ... etc. resemble each other. Admittedly, philosophers have talked in this way, and then, because such "resemblances" can be manufactured almost at will, have used the point in support of the dogma that any group of particulars must exhibit resemblances to each other. But the dogma is a philosopher's dogma which ordinary thought and discourse do not seem to accept.

The point may be backed up by asking whether ' ∼ P' applies, say to the particular *a*, in virtue of a relational or a non-relational property. It seems that it cannot be a matter of *a* standing in some relation to particulars which are P. For suppose that there had been no Ps and so, in our view, no property P. The predicate ' ∼ P' would still have applied to *a*. (It is a truth about every particular that it does not accelerate through the speed of light.) And if it applies to *a* in virtue of a non-relational property in the case where there are Ps, must it not apply in virtue of a non-relational property where there are no Ps? So *not being P*, if a property at all, must be a non-relational property of *a*. And now, once the suggestion that *not being P* is a relational property is out of the way, is it not pretty clear that, where *a* and *b* both lack P, they do not thereby possess a common (non-relational) feature?

Second, the admission of negative properties leads to a conclusion, noted by McTaggart (1921, § 62), that every particular must have exactly the same number of properties. For each particular, and for each positive property, the particular either has that property, or else lacks it and so has the corresponding negative property. We may therefore set up a one–one correlation between the class of properties possessed by any one particular and the class of properties possessed by any other particular. This result pleased McTaggart, but should appal any Empiricist. If we restrict properties to positive properties, then it becomes a matter to be decided *a posteriori*, if at all, whether two particulars have or have not the same number of properties. I suggest that this is a strong argument for restricting properties to positive properties.

McTaggart's argument is a very beautiful one, even if I am correct in thinking that the conclusion to be drawn from it is not McTaggart's. Edward Khamara has pointed out that it depends on the assumption that, for each particular and each property, the only two alternatives are that the particular has the property or that it has the corresponding negative property. But, he objects, there might be properties such that, if the particular falls in a certain "category", it neither has nor lacks that property. (Virtue is neither circular nor not circular.) Consider, then, two particulars in different categories.

There would be no assurance that they had the same number of properties.

But even if the assumption on which McTaggart's argument rests is denied, it would still yield the conclusion that two particulars in the same category must have the same number of properties. For, I assume, two particulars belong to the same category if and only if it makes sense to attribute to them properties within the same range of properties. So, given McTaggart's assumption that the absence of a positive property is a property, such particulars will have the same number of properties. An example of a category of particulars would, presumably, be ordinary physical things. To know *a priori* that all the particulars within such a category have the same number of properties would be to have more knowledge than it is easy to believe that we have!

Third, properties should be such that it at least makes sense to attribute causal powers to objects in virtue of these properties. But how could a mere lack or absence endow anything with causal powers? It is not an easy notion. Nothing will come of nothing! It is true that we are prepared to say such things as "Lack of water caused him to die". But do we take such remarks with ontological seriousness? Michael Tooley has pointed out that it seems to be ridiculous to say "Lack of poison caused him to remain alive." Yet if the two statements make an ontological claim at all, they make the same sort of claim. It appears that a practical interest in obtaining water in order to stay alive is all that lies behind the first statement.

An Occamist argument may be advanced against crediting negative properties, if they exist, with causal power. Suppose that we consider simply the positive properties (and relations) of the particulars involved in a certain situation. It will be for total science to determine just what these properties and relations are, to determine just which predicates correspond to genuine identities of nature. Science, in particular physics, has already gone far enough to show us in a rough general way what some of these universals will be. Now it seems that these properties and relations are all that are required in order to explain the causal outcome of the situation considered. Hence, we have no reason to attribute causal powers to the particulars in the situation in virtue of their lack of other positive properties and relations. As a further consequence, we have reason to deny that such lacks are genuine properties and relations.

Fourth, there is an argument suggested by Michael Tooley. It depends on the fact that disjunction is definable in terms of negation together with conjunction. Assume that if 'P' is a property-predicate, and '$\sim$P' has application, then '$\sim$P' is a property-predicate. Assume that if 'P' and 'Q' are property-predicates, then, if 'P&Q' has application, it too is a property-predicate. (This second assumption will be argued for in the next chapter.) Now consider a case in which 'P' and 'Q' are property-predicates and in which both '$\sim$P&$\sim$Q' and '$\sim$($\sim$P&$\sim$Q)' are predicates having application. Since '$\sim$P&$\sim$Q' has application, therefore '$\sim$P' and '$\sim$Q' have application; and since P and Q are properties, therefore $\sim$P and $\sim$Q are properties. Since '$\sim$P&$\sim$Q' has application, therefore $\sim P\&\sim Q$ is a property. Since '$\sim$($\sim$P&$\sim$Q)' has application, therefore $\sim(\sim P\&\sim Q)$ is a property. But this is logically equivalent to the "property" $P\vee Q$. We have, however, seen reason to reject disjunctive properties. Negative properties are suspect, but disjunctive properties are intolerable! So, granted that we have good reason to admit conjunctive properties, we have good reason to reject negative as well as disjunctive properties. This argument is strengthened by the contention, also to be argued for in the next chapter, that it is logically and epistemically possible that *every* property is a conjunctive property.

It may be suggested that our four arguments have not so much pointed to the conclusion that there are no negative properties as that there *need* not be negative properties. Suppose that there is one and only one property, Q, which particulars possess if and only if they lack P. Can we not say that *not being P* is, in this case, identical with the (positive) property, Q? Similar remarks may then be made about disjunctive properties.

With no great certainty, I am inclined to reject this compromise view. It is true that in such a case we can assert:

$$(x)\,(Qx \equiv \sim Px)$$

But I do not think that we should move from this to:

$$Q = \sim P.$$

We can form a predicate 'having the property possessed by those and only those particulars which do not have P'. This predicate will apply in virtue of the possession of Q. Predicates of this sort will be discussed in ch. 17, where they will be christened "external" predicates. But there is nothing in the semantics of such predicates which forces us to say that the predicate applies in virtue of *not being P*.

So there are reasons to reject negative properties. Those philosophers who have tried to solve the problem of evil by arguing that evil is privation, and privation is nothing, showed a sound metaphysical instinct, at least with respect to privations. Can we then produce a suitable correspondence-rule which will involve nothing but the sentence ' ~ Pa', on the one hand, and the object with its (positive) properties, on the other? If so, we remove the need to postulate negative properties.

Let us go back to the original, simple, case where 'Pa' corresponds to the world because *a* indeed has the property P. If *a* also has the property, Q, 'Pa' will fail to have *this* sort of correspondence to the state of affairs of *a*'s being Q. But the failure of simple correspondence must not hide the fact that 'Pa' does have a certain sort of correspondence to the state of affairs Qa. It may be compared to the sort of correspondence which exists between a photograph of A and a man B. Keith Campbell suggests that we call it "counter-correspondence". Counter-correspondence is a form of correspondence. It involves two terms and a rule which connects these terms. There might be a (trivial) game in which we paired off photographs and people according to the rule that the photograph must be a photograph of somebody else.

But now let us suppose that 'Pa' has this sort of correspondence, *viz.* counter-correspondence, not simply to Qa but to Ra and so on for *each* property *a* has. *a* must then *lack* property P. But now we understand the correspondence-rule for ' ~ Pa'. ' ~ Pa' corresponds if and only if for each property, ø such that øa, 'Pa' counter-corresponds to øa.

With this there vanishes the need to postulate negative properties and also, of course, negative states of affairs (negative facts). We get a correspondent for ' ~ Pa' without postulating that *a* has the property, *not being P*. The positive properties do the job instead. It is true that the argument has not proved that there are no negative properties and facts, but it does seem to eliminate the need for them.

It may be objected that the relation of counter-correspondence involves the very notion of negation which we are trying to get rid of. Given that *a* is P, 'Pa' bears a certain relation to the state of affairs Pa. Suppose *a* to be also Q, then 'Pa' stands to the state of affairs Qa in a way which can only be defined by saying that it depends upon the *absence* of the relation which 'Pa' bears to Pa. So, it may be said, we get rid of the negative property and negative states of affairs only to have them reappear in the correspondence-relation.

Two comments may be made in reply to this objection. First, this objection, like the parallel objection in the case of disjunctive predicates, misunderstands what the object of the argument has been. That object is not to give a reductive analysis of the proposition that *a* is not P. Such a task would be impossible of achievement. The object is simply to set up a semantic correlation between the sentence ' ~ Pa' and the states of affairs, Qa, Ra . . . etc. which will ensure the truth of the proposition that *a* is not P without appealing to negative properties or negative states of affairs. This, I hope, has been achieved. It would not matter if the notion of negation was used in describing this correlation, any more than it matters that the notion of disjunction is used to describe the correlation between the sentence '(PVQ)a' and the world when it is true that (PVQ)a.

But second, it is not clear that description of counter-correspondence involves invoking the absence of a *relation*, where a relation is taken to be a genuine universal. In stating the objection to my account of the correspondence of ' ~ Pa' to the world, I permitted myself use of the word 'relation', but not in developing the account itself. Where 'Pa' corresponds to the state of affairs Pa, a two-place predicate, 'corresponds', applies to the sentence-type 'Pa' and the state of affairs Pa. Where ' ~ Pa' corresponds to reality a two-place predicate, 'counter-corresponds', applies to the sentence-type 'Pa' taken along with each of the states of affairs Qa, Ra . . . etc. in an ordered pair. What genuine relations or what absence of genuine relations may be involved in these situations is a matter for deep and difficult investigation. In ch. 19 (Relations), it will be pointed out that it does not follow, just because a many-place predicate applies, that it automatically applies in virtue of a genuine relation holding between the particulars the predicate applies to.

A final note on the nature of the correspondence of ' ~ Pa' to the world. What of the case where '*a*' lacks reference (*a* does not exist)? It seems that the notion of counter-correspondence can be applied to referring expressions just as much as to sentences. Where '*a*' lacks reference it counter-corresponds to every object that there is. Again, a predicate may have counter-correspondence to all properties. An example of the latter would be the "empty" predicate 'bewitched'. In the case of a sentence like 'The present King of France is bewitched' referring expression and predicate will counter-correspond to all objects and all properties respectively.

To sum up. Wittgenstein said in the *Tractatus* that his fundamental thought was that the logical constants do not signify (4.0312). There is a sense in which, if our argument has been correct, the logical constants 'V' and ' ~ ' do not signify. For they do not tell us anything directly about what it is in the world which corresponds to the sentences and/or predicates of which they form a part. Instead, they tell us what correspondence-rules are to be adopted for other portions of these sentences and predicates.

Before ending this section, a word on the notion of *alteration*. When a thing alters, it gains or it loses some property or relation. It is generally assumed among contemporary philosophers that it is *ontologically* an arbitrary matter whether we say that a property (relation) was gained or lost. For we can say either that the thing ceased to be red, or that it came to be not-red. But now that we have rejected negative properties, and negative relations, this view cannot be accepted. There is a genuine *issue* whether a property or relation was gained or lost.

It might be maintained that whenever an object loses a property, it also gains another, and *vice versa*. Much alteration involves a thing losing a determinate property but acquiring another determinate property under the same determinable. In such a case, a property *is* both lost and gained. However, there seem to be cases where a determinate property is lost but no other determinate under the same determinable is gained. A coloured thing becoming transparent would be an example. It might still be held that some other property is gained, but I do not know how this proposition would be argued for.

# 15

# *Acceptance of conjunctive universals*

## 1 *Why conjunctive universals must be admitted*

Given that 'P' and 'Q' are property-predicates, applying in virtue of distinct properties, then, we have argued, 'P∨Q', '∼P' and '∼Q' are not property-predicates. By contrast it will be argued that, subject to one restricting condition, the conjunctive predicate 'P&Q' is a property-predicate. The restricting condition is simply the Principle of Instantiation: there must be at least one particular to which the predicate applies. There must be an $x$ such that Px and Qx. Thus, make the (almost certainly incorrect!) assumption that *rationality* and *animality* are both properties. Given that there are rational animals, *rationality-and-animality* will also be a property.

However, the admission of conjunctive properties (more broadly conjunctive universals) must not be misunderstood. There is no reason to postulate conjunctive properties *additional* to the properties which go to make up the conjunctive properties: the conjuncts. If $a$ has the property, P, and also has the distinct property, Q, then, I maintain, it has the conjunctive property P&Q. But this is not to say that $a$ has three wholly distinct properties, P, Q and *P&Q*. The blade of a knife is a thing, its handle is a thing and the whole knife is a thing. But this does not mean that there are three wholly distinct things: the blade, the handle and the knife.

The principle involved is that invoked by Nelson Goodman (see especially Goodman 1956), which he miscalls "Nominalism", the principle of not taking the very same individuals over again in different ways. Goodman, of course, uses the principle against classes. He denies that the various classes which can be formed from a given aggregate of individuals are entities over and above the original aggregate. But it can equally be invoked to prevent properties multiplying beyond reason. Indeed, Goodman's "Nominalist" principle is one which should be welcomed and embraced by the Realist about universals, if he is a sober Realist.

So conjunctive properties are not properties over and above their conjuncts. But, it may be asked, why should we admit conjunctive properties *at all?* Reinhardt Grossmann (1972, 1973) denies that there are conjunctive properties. His position is of great interest to our argument because he begins by *rejecting* a principle which he calls "the Principle of Property-Abstraction":

> there exists a property *g* which an entity e has *if and only if* . . . e . . . where the dots indicate any well-formed propositional context. (1972, p. 160)

This Principle resembles the principle which we, too, have rejected in ch. 13 § 1, that each distinct predicate applies to the objects it applies to in virtue of its own peculiar property and/or relation.

Grossmann uses his denial of the Principle of Property-Abstraction in a number of ways. First, he solves Russell's paradox about properties which have the "property", *not having themselves as one of their properties.* (It is the exact parallel of the more famous paradox about the class of all classes which are not members of themselves.) Grossmann agrees that there are properties of which it is *true* that they do not have themselves as one of their properties. But he denies that *not having themselves as one of their properties* is a property. In our terms, he denies that 'not having themselves as one of their properties' is a property-predicate. If negative properties are rejected, this must be accepted. But once this premiss is denied, he points out, the contradiction cannot be deduced.[1]

Second, he denies that Goodman's *grue* is a property. (A thing is grue if and only if it is green before a certain $t_1$ or blue after $t_1$.) In our terms, again, 'grue' is not a property-predicate. For suppose that 'grue' applies to an object, *a*, before $t_1$ and also after $t_1$. We are not *forced* to say that the predicate applies at the two times in virtue of something about the object *a* which is *identical.* And what we know of the world makes it fairly clear that in fact no such identical property is involved.

---

[1] The paradox of the class of all classes which are not members of themselves cannot be dissolved in this way. The classes which are not members of themselves do form a *class*. Michael Dunn has suggested to me that this is a defect in Grossmann's solution, on the ground that it is likely that both paradoxes invoke the same erroneous reasoning. But may it not be that the property-paradox involves at least *two* erroneous assumptions? One of these assumptions, the one uncovered by Grossmann, lacks a false counterpart in the case of the class-paradox. But both paradoxes may contain a further false assumption, assumptions which are counterparts of each other.

Third, given a class {a, b, c . . .}, Grossmann denies that there is a property, *being identical with a or with b or with c* . . . In our terms, 'identical with *a* or *b* or *c* . . .' is again not a property-predicate. It is not even an open predicate, nor is it a pure predicate.

But besides these interesting coincidences of doctrine with ours, there is also a major divergence. Grossmann also denies that there are conjunctive properties. Why does he do so? The reason is that he thinks that all properties are simple. If there were conjunctive properties, they would be complex.

I agree with Grossmann thus far. If every complex universal (complex property or relation) were a complex of simple universals then it would be rather natural to speak of the simple universals as *the* universals. But I do not think that it can be shown that every complex universal is a complex of simple universals. In the particular case of properties, it is logically and epistemically possible that all properties are conjunctive properties.

The following proposition seems to involve no contradiction. For all properties, P, there exists a property, Q, and a wholly distinct property, R, such that P = Q&R. Thus, make the unlikely supposition that *humanity, animality* and *rationality* are properties. Suppose further that *humanity* is the conjunction of *animality* and *rationality*. Why might not *animality* and *rationality* themselves be conjunctions of further distinct properties and so *ad infinitum*? An exact analogy with respect to particulars is the logical possibility that for all particulars, *x*, there should be wholly distinct particulars, *y* and *z*, which are proper parts of *x*. This latter principle is simply the infinite divisibility of particulars, generally accepted to be a coherent notion. An equally coherent notion, I suggest, is the *infinite resolubility* of properties into conjunctions of properties.

Nor is it a bare logical possibility that properties should be thus infinitely resoluble. It is an epistemic possibility. There seems to be nothing in what we know to rule out the possibility or even make it unlikely, though I know nothing to rule it in either. This being so, to maintain with Grossmann that there are no conjunctive properties, but only simple ones, leaves it logically and epistemically possible that there are no properties at all. I take this to be a good reason for rejecting Grossmann's view, and admitting conjunctive properties.

There are semantic and epistemological arguments which can be advanced against the possibility that all properties may be resolved *ad infinitum* into conjunctions of properties. The semantic argument is developed by McTaggart in more than one passage. For instance:

> it is beyond doubt that there are no compound characteristics except such as are composed of simple characteristics. Every quality and every relation must mean something [sic] so that when it is asserted that anything has that quality, or stands in that relation to anything, the assertion may be significant. And the meaning of a compound characteristic depends on the meaning of its parts. A compound characteristic, therefore, which had no simple parts, would involve a vicious infinite regress. (1921, p. 183)

McTaggart is arguing that because meanings cannot involve infinite semantic complexity, therefore characteristics cannot involve infinite complexity. But the argument obviously depends (yet again!) upon the old, bad, equation of universals with meanings which we have set our faces against in this work.

It is the Argument from Meaning which lies behind Logical Atomism. Meaning cannot be infinitely complex, so there must be simple atoms in the world to correspond to atoms of meaning. I find it heartening, however, that in later years one of the two great protagonists of Logical Atomism explicitly abandoned the doctrine. In *My Philosophical Development* (1959) Russell wrote:

> I believed, originally, with Leibniz, that everything complex is composed of simples, and that it is important in considering analysis to regard simples as our goal. I have come to think, however, that, although many things can be known to be complex, nothing can be *known* to be simple, and, moreover, that statements in which complexes are named can be completely accurate, in spite of the fact that the complexes are not recognized as complex. (pp. 165–6)

Russell here sums up, with his accustomed succinctness and cheerful disregard for his own earlier labours, the position which I wish to maintain. (He does not specifically apply his remarks to universals, but I do not suppose that he would reject the application.)

The epistemological argument for simple properties is a variant of the semantic argument. It starts from the premisses: (a) there are properties which we are aware of; (b) our minds are finite. If *these* properties, at least, were infinitely complex, it is argued, our finite minds would *not* be able to be aware of them.

But just as the semantic argument confuses semantic with ontological simplicity so this argument confuses epistemological with ontological simplicity. Since we are aware of properties and our minds are finite, there must be properties which we cannot analyse further, which are simple *for us*, which are epistemologically simple. But it does not follow that properties which "we clearly and distinctly perceive to be simple" are simple in fact, are ontologically simple. Why should we not react to a complex property in a simplistic manner? Indeed, going further, would it not be surprising if middle-sized objects like ourselves, with faculties adapted to discovering the biologically relevant natures of other middle-sized objects, should be capable of discerning directly the basic properties of the world, if there are any? If there are ultimate or atomic particulars out of which the world is constituted, we are not aware of them, at any rate in the state of nature. Equally if there are atomic properties, why should we expect to be aware of *them*? (The same will hold for relations, of course.)

In order to strengthen still further the case for admitting conjunctive properties, it will be helpful to contrast the admission of such properties with the hypothesis that there are disjunctive and negative properties.

First, we noted that it is implausible to say that in the case of disjunctive and negative "properties", there is something identical in all the objects in virtue of which the corresponding predicates apply. By contrast, if a number of particulars each have two properties, P and Q, it is perfectly natural to say that this constitutes a respect in which they are identical.

Second, we have seen that if disjunctive and negative properties are admitted, then we can draw *a priori* conclusions about the number of properties particulars can have. An Empiricist will think this "advantage" a disadvantage! Admission of conjunctive properties, however, allows no particular deductions about the number of properties that things have, at least when the admission is conjoined with the Principle of Instantiation. One result of admitting conjunctive properties is that it does become even more arbitrary just what is to count as *one* property. But this is not counter-intuitive. We talk of proper*ties*, but we need not think that they are like cows, to be numbered unambiguously. Particular*s* exhibit the same ambiguity. Is a blade with a handle one or two things? Is *being P&Q* one or two properties?

Third, we noticed that there was no natural link between disjunctive and negative "properties" and the causal powers of things. Suppose *a* has P but lacks Q. The predicate 'PVQ' applies to it. It may have causal powers in virtue of its *being P*. Nothing is added by the disjunctive "property", *P or Q*. But suppose that besides being P, *a* is also Q. Q may be expected to bestow additional causal powers upon *a*. It is worth noticing, also, as Lauchlan Chipman has pointed out to me, that what Q adds may not simply be the powers that Q by itself would bestow. The conjunctive property may bestow *more* or *less* than the sum of the causal powers bestowed by P and Q taken separately.

Finally, we have argued that it is logically possible that all properties are conjunctive properties. Could an upholder of negative properties maintain that it was logically possible that all properties be negative properties? Clearly not. Every particular must have some positive properties. Otherwise it would be a "bare particular". Could an upholder of disjunctive properties maintain that every property might be a disjunctive property? That is, could it be the case that for each property, P, there exist distinct properties, Q and R, such that P = QVR? I do not think so. Either none of these disjuncts will resemble each other, or some will. Suppose, first, that no disjuncts resemble each other. What justification can there be for treating as a *single* property something which dissolves forever into differences? The original "property" will lack a principle of unity and however far it is decomposed into disjuncts they too will lack a principle of unity. Such a world, it seems, would contain no properties. Suppose, second, that at some point we reach a disjunction of properties which have some resemblance. We have yet to discuss the important and difficult question of the resemblance of universals, a far more difficult matter than that of the resemblance of particulars. But I will argue in ch. 22 that the resemblance of universals is normally a matter of their having a common, that is identical, *part*. (The alternative is that the universals have a common property.) Such a part of a property will be a property itself, and *it* cannot be disjunctive if the resemblance of the original properties is to be real. So, I maintain, the resemblance of the disjuncts covertly contradicts the hypothesis that all properties are disjunctive. Hence it seems that an upholder of disjunctive properties could not maintain that every property was disjunctive, which contrasts once again with the meaningful hypothesis that every property is conjunctive.

Three further points should be made before concluding this section. First, parallel to the notion of the infinite divisibility of particulars is the notion of their infinite extensibility. It is logically possible that every particular is a proper part of some larger (perhaps scattered) particular. Similarly, parallel to the notion of the infinite resolubility of conjunctive properties is the notion of their infinite composition. There is no contradiction in the notion that, for all properties, P, there exists a wholly distinct property, Q, such that *P&Q* is a property (pleonastically: instantiated property). Whether or not these possibilities are realized is a question about which a philosopher has no special expertise, although perhaps nobody else has either. But it is an important part of the philosophical enterprise to enlarge our sense of the possibilities in nature. Alas, it is a portion of the enterprise which contemporary philosophers are all too inclined to leave to others, such as physicists.

Second, conjunctive properties may or may not be "accidental" conjunctions. That is to say, it may or may not be the case that the conjuncts are in some way nomically connected.

Third, it may be noted that, if an instantiated conjunction of properties is a property, then the conjunction of all the properties of a particular (its "nature") is a property. If we further hold that, for each property, it is logically possible that it should be multiply instantiated, then it cannot be the case that the Identity of Indiscernibles is a necessary truth.

## II *The notions of whole and part*

We have said that the property, P, is not wholly distinct from the conjunctive property, P&Q. P stands to P&Q as the blade of a knife stands to the whole knife. What we have in both cases is a part of a whole.

Consider the following pairs:

| | |
|---|---|
| New South Wales | Australia |
| The Terror | The French Revolution |
| an abstract particular (the "visual cube") | the concrete particular (the cube) |
| the class of women | the class of human beings |
| the class of even numbers | the class of natural numbers |
| the proposition that p | the proposition that p&q |
| the property P | the property P&Q |

It is sometimes thought that the notion of part and whole has a special link with *space* and so a special link with the first pair on our list. I believe that this is an error. Spatial parts and wholes are simply the cases of part and whole which most easily strike the imagination. I suggest that in each of the pairs listed above, the left-hand member stands to the right-hand member as part to whole. In the case of the two sets of classes it is customary to speak of a sub-class of a class (or sub-set of a set). But this, I think, is simply a case of part and whole where part and whole are both classes (sets). Similar remarks apply to the other pairs on the list.

If this is correct, then the apparent relation of part and whole is extraordinarily ubiquitous. I believe that there is a simple explanation for this. It is as ubiquitous as the "relations" of *identity* and *difference* because part and whole is one of the two cases of *partial identity* or, if you like, *partial difference*.

We may illustrate by considering spatial cases. Australia is strictly identical with the smallest continent. It is completely distinct from (strictly different from) Europe. But strict identity or strict difference of spatial objects does not always obtain, though it is easy to overlook the intermediate cases. There are two sorts of intermediate case. Two adjoining terrace houses are not identical, but they are not completely distinct from each other either. They are partially identical, and this partial identity takes the form of having a common part. Australia and New South Wales are not identical, but they are not completely distinct from each other. They are partially identical, and this partial identity takes the form of the whole–part "relation". It is clear that parallel examples can easily be manufactured for the other sorts of pairs illustrated on our list.

Partial identity admits of at least rough-and-ready degree. Begin with New South Wales and then take larger and larger portions of Australia. One is approaching closer and closer to complete identity with Australia. Parallel examples in other categories are again easily manufactured.

Philosophers are familiar with the philosophical puzzles which cluster around the notion of identity. In particular, they have come to see that there are problems in treating it as a relation. If it is correct to say that the whole–part "relation" is a particular case of partial identity, then we may expect to find that the notion of whole and part is involved in the same sort of problems as the notion of identity. If the "relations" of overlap and whole–part are cases of partial identity, then the so-called "calculus of individuals" together with "mereology" are simply developments of the logic of identity.

However, there is an obstacle which makes it a little harder to see that P is a part of P&Q than in the other cases of part and whole. The class of particulars which have the property, P&Q, may well be a proper part of the class of Ps and also of the class of Qs. The same goes for the corresponding aggregates. But this is simply a manifestation of the so-called "inverse variation of intension and extension". P, and Q, remain parts of P&Q. A similar situation arises with overlap, that is, properties (or relations) with a common part. Suppose that both P&Q and Q&R are properties. They have a common part, Q. Yet the class of P&Qs and the class of Q&Rs may be a proper part of the class of Qs, and the class of P&Q&Rs may be an empty one.

If identity is not a relation, then *standing as whole to part* and *overlapping* must also come under suspicion, because they involve partial identity. Nevertheless, where the identity is only partial, genuine relations are involved. Consider, again, the two conjunctive properties, P&Q and Q&R. The properties, P and R, are genuinely related. They have the relation of *entering into a conjunction with the same property*. More formally, there exists a particular, $x$, and a particular, $y$, and a property, ø, such that $x$ is P and $x$ is ø and $y$ is R and $y$ is ø. In Chapter 24 we shall be discussing whether universals can stand in second-order relations to each other. *Entering into a conjunction with the same property* is not a second-order relation between properties. A purely first-order analysis of it has just been given. Nevertheless, it is a genuine relation between universals, capable of multiple instantiation, but holding in this instance between P and R.

It will emerge in later chapters that the notion of partial identity is of immense importance and value in solving problems in the theory of universals. It seems that it can be extended to what will be called "structural" properties. Suppose that there is a property, O, which is a matter of a part of the thing which is O having property P and standing in a relation of the sort R to the remainder of the thing which is O, a remainder which has the property, Q. This is a structural property. P, Q and R are all parts of this property in the usual sense of "part".

There is a further obstacle to the recognition that such properties and relations are *parts* of structural properties. It is easy to give rather unthinking assent to the following principle:[1]

*If F is a property, and G is a property which is part of that property, then whatever particulars have F also have G.

The principle holds for conjunctive properties. If there is a property, P&Q, then P and also Q are properties of all those particulars which have the conjunctive property. We may therefore speak of the *Conjunction Principle*. If we can equate Frege's *concepts* with properties, then we find Frege (1884) giving passing assent to the Principle in the second sentence of the following passage:

> By properties which are asserted of a concept I naturally do not mean the characteristics [Merkmale] which make up the concept. These latter are properties of the things which fall under the concept, not of the concept. Thus "rectangular" is not a property of the concept "rectangular triangle" . . . (Section 53)

For the case of structural properties, however, the Conjunction Principle breaks down. Suppose that *being O* is a matter of something which is P having R to something which is Q. It may well be the case that Os are not Ps or Qs. Os will have *parts* which are Ps and *parts* which are Qs, but will not *be* Ps or be Qs.

The Conjunction Principle could be used to argue that in such a case P, Q and R are not parts of O. But it seems to me that the obvious moral to draw is that the Conjunction Principle is false. Parts of a property may qualify different particulars from those which the property qualifies.

III *Strictly universal predicates and truth-functions*

Given that 'P' and 'Q' are indeed property-predicates, applying solely in virtue of a single property, then we have concluded that 'PVQ' and '~P' are not property-predicates. For 'P&Q' to be a property-predicate an instantiation condition must be met. There must be (at some time) a particular, $x$, to which the predicate 'P&Q' applies. However, if the instantiation condition holds, then 'P&Q' is a property-predicate.

---

[1] Here, and henceforward, an asterisk will be used to mark principles which are rejected.

But what, it may be asked, of *other* truth-functional connectives of 'P' and 'Q'?

We may start by laying down a plausible general principle: the *Principle of Logical Equivalence*. As a first formulation of this we may try:

> *If predicates are logically equivalent, then they apply, where they do apply, in virtue of the very same property or properties (relation or relations).

However, Michael Tooley has pointed out that this definition is exposed to counter-example. Suppose that *a* has distinct properties, F and G. The predicates 'FV ~ F' and 'GV ~ G' are logically equivalent, yet the first predicate applies to *a* in virtue of its possession of the property, F, the second in virtue of its possession of G.

The difficulty arises from the logical equivalence of any two necessary truths. This suggests that we should exclude from the scope of the Principle predicates which logically must apply to any object. (These constitute an uninteresting set of predicates, in any case, from our point of view. We may call them predicates which are *logically empty*. They are a sub-species of empty predicate. See ch. 13 § IV.) The Principle of Logical Equivalence then becomes:

> If predicates are logically equivalent, but not logically empty, then they apply, where they do apply, in virtue of the very same property or properties (relation or relations).

The principle may be supported in the following way. Why do such logically equivalent predicates necessarily apply to exactly the same particulars? The obvious explanation is that they apply in virtue of the very same universal (or disjunctive range of universals in the case of predicates which are not strictly universal predicates). Suppose, contrary to the Principle, that 'P' and 'Q' are logically equivalent, but not logically empty, predicates, yet they apply in virtue of distinct properties, *being P* and *being Q*. What evidence could there ever be that two properties were involved? There is not even the logical possibility of an object which has the one property but lacks the other. As will be argued at greater length in the next chapter, difference of property can only be detected where that difference bestows difference of causal power. But no procedure can be specified which will sort out the relative causal contributions of the necessarily co-extensive properties, *being P* and *being Q*.

It may be noticed that it is easy and natural to pass from the principle that logically equivalent predicates which are not logically empty apply in virtue of the very same universal(s) or range of universals to what might be called the Intensional Principle:

*If predicates are *not* logically equivalent, and are not logically empty, then they cannot apply, where they do apply, in virtue of the very same property or properties (relation or relations).

(If logically empty predicates had been allowed, then one predicate might be 'FV ~ F', another 'F', and both predicates applicable to *a* in virtue of *a*'s property F.)

The transition from the Principle of Logical Equivalence to the Intensional Principle is, however, obviously invalid. Furthermore, the Intensional Principle, even when restricted to predicates which are not logically empty, is in fact false. In the next chapter we will see that while predicates which are not logically empty *must*, the same sort of predicates when not logically equivalent *may* or *may not*, apply in virtue of the very same universals. It is this which permits the so-called "contingent identification of properties".

Should we say that predicates which are logically equivalent but not logically empty are the same predicate? Our criterion of identity for predicates is semantic, so to say this will have the consequence that such predicates have the same meaning. This seems a harsh thing to have to say when we consider such cases as the counter-intuitive equivalences which are sometimes met with in difficult logical investigations. However, I see no real objection to speaking in this way. The conclusion that meaning-equivalences may be opaque to the intellect is not really all that hard to accept once we have overcome Cartesian prejudices about the clearness and distinctness of our knowledge of meaning. Any philosopher who thinks that there is such a thing as "conceptual analysis" can hardly deny that argument may bring to light equivalences of meaning which are rather a surprise to us.

So we shall take it that, for instance, 'P' and ' ~ ~P', provided that they are not logically empty, not only apply in virtue of exactly the same universals but are in fact the same predicate.

We can now give a simple rule for truth-functional compounds of property-predicates. Such a predicate is itself a property-predicate if and only if (a) the instantiation condition is satisfied, (b) it is logically equivalent to a property-predicate *or* it is logically equivalent to a conjunction of predicates each of which is a property-predicate. Given this rule, if 'P' and 'Q' are both property-predicates, 'P ⊃ Q', '∼P∨Q' and '∼(P&Q)', for instance, will be denied to be property-predicates, which is surely the result which we want. '∼(∼P∨∼Q)' however is a property-predicate, providing it applies, because it is logically equivalent to 'P&Q'.

A parallel rule will apply in the case of relation-predicates. In the case of relations, however, it will often be necessary to put the point not in terms of universals, but of *states of affairs*. Although 'R' and 'R̆' are not always logically equivalent predicates, 'Rab' is logically equivalent to 'R̆ba'. *a*'s having R to *b* is logically equivalent to *b*'s having the converse of R to *a*. There is therefore just one state of affairs in virtue of which the two sentences correspond to reality, if they do correspond. (Just as we say that the logically equivalent predicates must not be logically empty so we must stipulate that the logically equivalent propositions expressed by the sentences must not themselves be necessary propositions.) It follows that there are not *two* relations, R and its converse, involved in the state of affairs, but only one. This one relation is what the Scholastics called the *fundamentum relationis*.

The argument of this section seems of the greatest importance for the theory of logical necessity. If logically equivalent predicates which are not logically empty apply in virtue of the very same universals, and logically equivalent propositions which are not themselves logically necessary are true in virtue of the very same state of affairs, then some *de dicto* account of logical necessity must be correct. The logical necessity of propositions must, in some way, derive from the words or concepts in which the propositions are expressed.

# 16

## The identification of universals

"sed forma non cognoscitur nisi ex operationibus"
Scotus (quoted Goodwin, 1961, p. 482)

### 1 Identity-conditions for universals

We have rejected disjunctive and negative universals but have accepted conjunctive ones. Indeed, it was argued that it is logically and even epistemically possible that every universal should be a conjunctive one.

However, the argument was deliberately kept at an abstract level. It was contended that there were universals but no examples were given. This apparent lack of empiricism springs from empiricism! Our Realism about universals is not, as many previous theories of universals have been, an *a priori* or Rationalist theory. Rather it draws its inspiration from the natural sciences and is prepared to be taught by theory and experience what universals there are. Identifications of universals must therefore be speculative. We might suggest that $e$, the electric charge of the electron, is such a (monadic) universal, because this charge is supposed to be *identical* in every electron. But later theory may come to deny that all electrons have exactly the same charge. (And we shall see reasons in ch. 22 to deny that *having some charge* is a genuine universal.)

Nevertheless, it may still be possible to give formal marks which we use in picking out universals and marking them off from each other. In particular, as already suggested at a number of points in our argument, there is a link between universals and *causality*. In what follows I will first restrict myself to monadic universals or properties and afterwards make some brief remarks extending what has been said to polyadic universals or relations.

I suggest that (a) the active and passive powers of particulars are determined by their properties. (b) Every property bestows some active and/or passive power upon the particulars of which it is a property. (c) A property bestows the very same power upon any particular of which it is a property. (d) Each different property bestows a different power upon the particulars of which it is a property. Each of these four propositions can, I think, be made plausible, although in the case of the last three the justification will be pragmatic only.

The first contention is that the active and passive causal powers of particulars are determined by the properties of the particulars. This follows from the not quite uncontroversial, but surely plausible, premiss that causal connections, whatever else they involve, involve law-like connections. (This premiss does not entail the Humean view, which I take to be false, that causation is mere constant conjunction. See ch. 24.) For a law-like connection is a connection subject to general rule, and so must depend upon the general nature, that is, the properties, of the particulars subject to the rule. Hence the causal powers of particulars are determined by their properties.

As already noted in ch. 14, such remarks as "Lack of water caused his death" create a *prima facie* difficulty for this first contention. For here the outcome of a certain situation appears to depend not upon the properties of the particulars involved but upon the absence from the situation of a thing with certain properties. Yet such absences, we have argued, are not properties of the situation. However, when we reflect a little on such cases, we are very ready to admit that the actual causal processes involved proceed solely in virtue of the (positive) properties of the situation. To say that lack of water caused his death reflects not a metaphysic of the causal efficacy of absences but merely ignorance. Certain (positive) processes were going on in his body, processes which, in the absence of water, resulted in a physiological condition in virtue of which the predicate 'dead' applied to his body. It is ignorance of the exact nature of these processes and conditions, or else it is just a convenient shorthand, which makes us speak instead of 'lack of water' as the cause.

The second contention is that every property bestows some active and/or passive power upon the particulars which it is a property of. It must be conceded here that it seems possible to conceive of a property of a thing which bestows neither active nor passive power of any sort. But if there are any such properties, then we can have absolutely no reason to suspect their existence. For it is only in so far as properties bestow powers that they can be detected by the sensory apparatus or other mental faculty. The supposition that there are such properties is like the supposition of an omnipotent all-deceiving Demon. Both suppositions may be logical possibilities, but they are possibilities which we can never have the slightest reason to think actualities.

So we are at least pragmatically justified in accepting the principle that every property bestows some power.

It may be noticed in passing that it seems possible to conceive of properties which bestow upon particulars active powers alone or passive powers alone. Properties of the first sort would be, as it were, "unmoved movers", while properties of the second sort would be "epiphenomenal". Whether we could ever have reason to believe in the existence of such causal one-way streets in the sphere of properties is a most difficult question. But, fortunately, our present purposes do not seem to require that we come to a decision about the question.

The third condition is that a property bestows the very same powers upon every particular which it is a property of. This proposition may be defended pragmatically by the consideration that, if the same property bestowed variable power upon different particulars, then we could have absolutely no way of judging that the different particulars have the same property. If things act differently in the same circumstances, then we attribute to them a different nature. To this pragmatic defence of the third condition will be added a deeper justification in Part Seven.

The fourth, and final, condition is that each different property must bestow different powers. The proposition is again defended pragmatically. It seems abstractly possible that two different properties should bestow exactly the same powers. However, in such a case, we could never have any good reason to think that the properties were distinct. The difference would be completely undetectable.

Our four propositions may be thought of as a set of identity-conditions for properties, identity-conditions which for the most part can only be pragmatically justified. (In a wider sense, the whole theory of universals being developed in this book is an attempt to provide identity-conditions for properties and relations.) The four propositions stand in close relation to, and are indeed inspired by, the "mark of being" offered by the Eleatic Stranger in Plato's *Sophist*:

I suggest that anything has real being, that is so constituted as to possess any sort of power either to affect anything else or to be affected, in however small a degree, by the most insignificant agent, though it be only once. I am proposing as a mark to distinguish real things, that they are nothing but power. (247d-e)

I have in effect appealed to the Stranger's "mark of being" in ch. 12. I there defended the world-hypothesis that what there is consists of nothing but propertied particulars standing in relations to each other. Against the suggestion that the world might contain, *in addition* to these entities, such things as possibilities, timeless propositions, and "abstract" classes, I argued that these latter entities had no causal power; and that if they had no power there was no good reason to postulate them. It was remarked at the end of that chapter that things have the causal powers they have in virtue of their properties (and relations). All that is now being done is to use the "mark of being" to exclude properties which bestow no power, and also to exclude different properties which fail to bestow different powers.

It may be objected that our marks of a property involve circularity, in particular that conditions (c) and (d) are circular. It was argued that a property always bestows the same powers and that different properties bestow different powers. But to talk of the same and different powers is to talk of the nature of the outcome which things having these properties have the power to produce in various circumstances. And what can the reference to *nature* be if it is not a reference to properties (and perhaps relations) of the affected particulars?

The point must be conceded, but I do not think that the circularity is vicious. It would be vicious if our identity-conditions were taken to be *definitions* of sameness and difference of property. In fact, however, the notions of sameness and difference of property are far too fundamental to be defined. (It is the error of Nominalism and also of Platonic Realism to attempt such a definition.) Cats cannot be defined as the offspring of two cats but it is a truth about cats that they are so engendered. And so it may be a truth about properties that the same property always bestows the same powers upon particulars and that different properties bestow different powers. These truths might then provide identity-conditions. It is true that these propositions would not serve to identify properties if we had no knowledge of properties (and hence sameness of property) in the first place. But it is quite wrong to demand that identity-conditions serve to dispel such radical ignorance. It is enough if identity-conditions give us a formal criterion for sameness and difference of property. They do not have to pick out properties for us, and they can employ the notion of property in the statement of the criterion.

It remains to extend our identity-conditions for properties to relations. Suppose that we consider the simplest case of two objects which stand in a certain relation. It seems reasonable to hold that at least some of the powers which the two objects have for joint action depend not only upon their properties but also upon the nature of their relation. It seems further reasonable to hold that each relation which the two particulars have bestows some power for joint action upon them. If this is not so, there will be no way in which such a relation could ever be detected. Again, the one relation must bestow the same powers for joint action upon any particulars it relates. If it did not, there would be no way of judging that the relation was the same. Finally, each different relation must bestow a different power of joint action. If they did not, the difference would be undetectable. This extension of the doctrine of identity-conditions to relations or polyadic universals seems to involve no difficulty.

In conclusion it may be noted that our identity-conditions assort nicely with the claim that there are certain (pure) predicates which apply to particulars but which do not apply in virtue of any universal or universals. For instance, it is true of every particular that it is identical with itself, but it was argued that to this pure predicate 'identical with itself' no property corresponds. Now we would not be inclined to think that *being identical with itself* bestowed any causal power upon particulars.

## II *Where do we start?*

Universals, then, are linked with powers of the particulars which have the properties or relations, different universals bestowing each their different power. But we have already seen that this will not solve the problem of identifying universals in the first place. Given a start, the identity-conditions may give formal conditions for going on. But how is the start to be made? 

Universals are linked with powers, and powers may be powers to act or be acted upon by any sort of thing whatsoever. However, we have access to the properties and relations of things only in so far as (a) the things act upon us, in particular upon our sensory apparatus; and (b) as a result we are disposed to classify certain particulars as all being alike in a certain respect.

Here we may turn once more to Anthony Quinton's position in his article "Properties and Classes" (1957, and see also 1973, ch. 9). Quinton distinguishes between those classes of particulars which are, and those which are not, *natural*. Natural classes, he says, are:

> of such a kind that people who are introduced to a few of the members can go on to pick out others without hesitation or idiosyncrasy . . . (p. 47)

Naturalness of class is a matter of degree:

> The amount of hesitation and idiosyncrasy will obviously vary in degree and there is no definite point at which there is just enough of them for us to pronounce a class arbitrary. (p. 47)

Again:

> To say that where pins have a common property games have only a family resemblance is to say that the class of pins is more natural than the class of games, that we can learn to recognize pins more surely and rapidly than we learn to recognize games. "Eulb" [not-blue] is artificial relative to blue for we should need more specimen instances in order to learn how to use it. (p. 58)

As we have already noted in ch. 4, Quinton is a (moderate) Class Nominalist who takes the existence of classes with different degrees of naturalness, in the sense just explained, to be an ultimate fact. We however seek to give an account of natural classes in terms of the properties of their members, or, in the case of classes of ordered pairs etc., in terms of relations between the pairs. But, while allowing for this disagreement with Quinton, he is correct in saying that, in seeking to identify properties and relations, it is our natural classifications which we must *start* with. Indeed, there is nowhere else to start. Certain things act upon us, and we classify them. By causing us to classify them, they manifest a similarity of power. So we judge that their properties (or relations) are at least similar.

How should we interpret degrees of naturalness? In ch. 13 § IV, pure predicates were classified under five headings. These headings were intended to capture different degrees on a single scale. At the top of the scale were "strictly universal" predicates, which apply to particulars in virtue of the one, identical, universal. The other degrees on the scale are fallings away from this strict standard of identity. Next came "homogeneous" predicates, which apply where the particular in question falls under one of a class of universals, but where the class is held together by a unitary general formula of a purely formal or topic-neutral sort. The predicate 'having a mass' is a plausible example, although discussion of such classes of properties as the class of the different masses must wait until ch. 22. A further falling away from identity is found with "family" predicates, of which 'game' seems a likely example. The class of universals involved "form a family", in the sort of way that Wittgenstein explained, but the class does not have that unified formal structure associated with homogeneous predicates. After family predicates come "heterogeneous" predicates, which apply in virtue of membership of a class of universals, a class which is not unified in any way. 'Either a raven or a writing-desk' and 'not a raven' would be examples. For the purposes of discussing Quinton's degrees of naturalness of classes, we can omit consideration of the fifth class of "empty" predicates.

I now suggest that we simply interpret Quinton's degrees of naturalness of classes as a matter of position on our scale. At the top come classes of particulars involving a single universal. Then come classes of particulars where the universals involved form a closely-knit, closely-resembling, class. To these succeed cases where the universals have a much looser resemblance and, finally, those cases where the universals involved are heterogeneous. The shades of blue have *more in common* than the properties which made for pinhood and gamehood, which in turn have more in common than that very heterogeneous assemblage, the universals which are not shades of blue.

So far, Quinton's doctrine of degree of naturalness of classes has simply been re-interpreted in terms of degrees of resemblance of universals. As we may put it, a certain transformation has been applied to his theory. But now we must be more critical. Although the identification of universals must begin with those classifications of things which we find natural, it is important to see, what Quinton seems not to admit, that these aboriginal classifications are not sacrosanct. Different sorts of causes may produce the same effect. A common effect upon the human classificatory system may be produced as a result of different properties or relationships of the particulars acting upon us. (I am not going back on the point made in § 1 that different universals must bestow difference of power. See the next paragraph but one.) As a result, our first classifications may involve mistakes. And even where no actual mistake is involved, the original classifications may be shown to rest upon relatively trivial resemblances which are replaced, when the scientific enterprise gets under way, by quite different and much more significant classifications. In general, what Quinton omits to note is that the *original* classifications can be subjected to criticism.

Such criticism must have a bootstrap character because we have nothing with which to criticize the classifications which we are naturally disposed to make except further classifications which we are naturally disposed to make. The ship must be rebuilt at sea from its own timbers (to coin a phrase). Nevertheless, the job can be done. Quinton's "natural classes" correspond to what Wilfrid Sellars calls "the manifest image of the world" and perhaps still more closely to the narrower Quinean conception of our "innate quality space". The natural classes are, and must be, the first word about the classification of things. But they need not be the last. The primitively natural scheme of classification is open to revision. Such revision may take the form of declaring that certain primitively "natural" classes lack a genuine unity, or that certain primitively "unnatural" classes possess genuine unity.

Such criticism of natural classifications stands in no contradiction to the notion argued for in § 1 that sameness of universals is linked with sameness of power and difference of universals with difference of power. Things with little or no resemblance may be classified together by the human classifier. Different sorts of things can affect us in the same way. But we only conclude that the things lack resemblance despite their appearance of possessing it, if a difference of effect brought about by different members of the natural class shows up *somewhere*. Property, P, and distinct property, Q, may bestow the same powers, or much the same powers, in circumstances of the sort C. But there will be other sorts of circumstance where P and Q bestow powers to produce different effects. Furthermore, if the classifier is to be aware of this difference of effects he must somehow record it, and so in the end the difference must have its effect upon him.

We may finish this section by considering some miscellaneous examples where the "natural" classifications may have to be abandoned.

An interesting case where perception appears to exaggerate the degree of disjunctiveness is that of heat and cold. To perception, heat and cold appear as two distinct ranges of qualities. But science and even common-sense gives us reason to think that only a single homogeneous range of qualities is involved.

Cases can be found where a predicate appears to apply to a natural class but turns out to be covertly negative. A pleasant example is given by Plato: the term "barbarian" as employed by the Greeks of his day. In the *Politicus* he speaks of:

> The kind of mistake a man would make who, seeking to divide the class of human beings into two, divided them into Greeks and Barbarians. This is a division most people in this part of the world make. They separate the Greeks from all other nations making them a class apart; thus they group all other nations together as a class, ignoring the fact that it is an indeterminate class made up of people who have no intercourse with each other and speak different languages. Lumping all this non-Greek residue together, they think it must constitute one real class because they have a common name 'barbarian' to attach to it. (262d)

Of course, since 'the Greeks' is a referring expression, 'barbarian' is not even a *pure* predicate, much less a strictly universal predicate.

This quotation is all the more interesting in view of the well-known passage in the *Republic* (already quoted in ch. 7 § 1):

> shall we proceed as usual and begin by assuming the existence of a single essential nature or Form for every set of things which we call by the same name? (595)

This procedure would have yielded a Form of Barbarian. But between the time of writing the *Republic* and writing the *Politicus* Plato appears to have learnt to reject negative universals and, with them, any simple scheme of correspondence between predicates and universals. (As argued in ch. 7 I take the *Republic* passage not to be an anticipation of the bad modern Argument from Meaning but an incautious, because linguistic, formulation of the One over Many argument.)

A more controversial example of the same sort is provided by the predicate 'black'. Let two assumptions be made which I believe to be both true but which are certainly controversial, especially if conjoined. The first is that the *experienced* quality of blackness is a property not of sensations but of physical objects, in particular, of their surfaces. The second is the scientific identification of colours with the sorts of wave-length emitted from the coloured surface. Given these assumptions, black surfaces turn out to be, as a matter of scientific fact, surfaces which do not emit any light. So the predicate 'black', apparently a positive predicate, applies in virtue of a certain lack or absence in the particulars to which it applies. The Pythagorean identification of "black night" with nothingness would thus turn out to be justified.

The discussion of the last three chapters has had as its main concern cases where one predicate applies in virtue of a disjunctive multiplicity of universals, universals which may lack any particular resemblance. We now pass on to consider cases, already adumbrated in the discussion of *blackness*, where two or more predicates apply to particulars in virtue of exactly the same universal or disjunctive set of universals. This will be the business of the next chapter.

# 17

## *Different semantic correlations between predicates and universals*

It will be argued in this chapter not only that different (non-synonymous) predicates may apply to particulars in virtue of the very same universals, or disjunctive range of universals, but also that such predicates may apply *in different semantic fashions*. Three such fashions will be distinguished. We examine first the distinction between predicates which merely "name" and predicates which "analyse" the corresponding universal or range of universals. After that, we will consider "external" predicates. It is convenient to treat our three sorts of predicate as sub-species of pure open predicates, although similar distinctions might be drawn in the case of other sorts of predicate. The classification of such predicates in this chapter cuts right across the classification already given in ch. 13 § IV.

Suppose that a certain universal is complex. It might, for instance, be a conjunctive universal. Suppose, further, that human beings notice that certain particulars fall under this universal and that they correlate a predicate with it. Suppose, however, that this complex universal is apprehended in a totalistic or *gestaltist* way so that users of the predicate are unable to resolve this universal in any way. For them, the universal is unanalysable. It is epistemologically simple for them. Such a predicate will be called a "naming" predicate. It need not be, is indeed very unlikely to be, a strictly universal predicate, because it may apply in virtue of a whole disjunctive range of universals. But, as I will use the term, to be a naming predicate the predicate in question must be a pure predicate and an open predicate. Where a predicate is a naming predicate, the way it is correlated with its universal or range of universals is obviously not the way in which a proper name is correlated with the thing it names. But there is a clear analogy. In both cases the word is functioning as a tag or label.

A naming predicate might apply to particulars in virtue of an ontologically simple universal. No analysing predicate could then apply. However, in the case we have just specified in the previous paragraph, the universal is complex. So not only a naming but also an analysing predicate is applicable. A predicate is an analysing one if and only if it spells out that complexity, partially or wholly.

In the case specified the universal is complex but is not apprehended as complex. Some philosophers seem to find such a situation difficult to understand. They would probably concede that we sometimes have the capacity to recognize a property or relation while lacking any very clear idea of the exact structure of the universal in question. But they seem to cling to the notion that in such cases we still have *some* grasp of the structure. We still know that the universal involves elements of certain general sorts, or, failing all else, know barely that the property is complex. Furthermore, I suspect, these philosophers cannot shake off the idea that at some deeper, more unconscious, level the mind is in possession of the exact formula and is able to tick off the relevant constituents of the universal in a way that the conscious mind cannot do.

Now it is true that in many cases we do have a vague grasp of the nature of complex universals, or disjunctive ranges of universals, although unable to make clear to ourselves the exact nature of the complexity involved. Furthermore, it is an intelligible hypothesis that at a deeper, unconscious, level some mental or purely physiological process goes on whereby the properties and relations involved in the complex are individually discriminated and checked off against a formula before attributions of the complex universals are made. But none of this is *necessary*. It is perfectly possible that (a) a universal is complex; (b) particulars falling under this universal act (in virtue of this universal) upon our sense-organs in an all-or-nothing way. We might register the presence of particulars falling under this universal without being able to analyse the universal in any way, either at a conscious or an unconscious level. We would then have a "simple idea" of a complex universal. If we introduce a predicate to correspond to this property, the predicate is a naming predicate.

Now, although the senses might thus fail to inform us about the structure of a universal, the structure might nevertheless become known or be guessed. Scientific investigation and argument, including high-level theoretical considerations, might lead to the conclusion that what is being reacted to at the sensory level as simple is in fact complex. The complexity may ultimately be correctly specified in a formula. The formula is a predicate. It is obviously not the same predicate as the original naming predicate because the predicates are not synonymous. But it applies to exactly the same particulars in virtue of exactly the same universal or range of universals as the naming predicate. The new predicate will be an *analysing* predicate. It may analyse to a lesser or greater depth.

The universals or range of universals detected by chicken-sexers, wine-tasters, and so on, may be cases in point. But I will not discuss such cases in detail. The controversial nature of the cases means that they have a tendency to confuse rather than clarify the situation. In any case, a thorough discussion of them would be of inordinate length. But I will note that I believe that the "secondary qualities" – colour, sound, taste, smell, heat, cold, etc. – fit the situation just sketched. Epistemologically, these qualities are simple. The uninstructed perceiver cannot analyse them. But there is good scientific reason to believe that they are in fact complex physical properties (more accurately, ranges of such properties) whose property-formula can be given, in theory at least, solely within the vocabulary of physics.

One interesting point which arises here is that such analysing predicates, if successfully arrived at, could cast light upon problems about the relation of properties which cannot be solved at the level of mere naming predicates. A no doubt trivial example is the relation of tastes, in particular sweet and sour. In the case of different colours we appear to be directly aware of their incompatibility. We are aware that the very same particular cannot possess two different colours. This incompatibility appears to be a necessary one and appears to be explained after the scientific identification of different colours with light of different wave-lengths. In the "state of nature" we are aware only that there is an incompatibility. In the light of the scientific identifications we learn just what the nature of the incompatibility is. But is it logically impossible for the very same thing to be sweet and sour? (I assume the truth of a Direct Realist theory of taste: tastes are properties of objects, not of our sensations.) The phenomenology of the situation where one tastes a sweet-and-sour dish is not at all clear. Unlike the incompatibility of colours it is hard to decide whether the situation is one where sweet but not sour things are mixed up together with sour but not sweet things, or whether the *very same thing* is both sweet and sour. Suppose, however, that we arrive at analysing predicates which could replace the naming predicates 'sweet' and 'sour'. The formulae for the two ranges of properties may then settle the question whether or not *sweetness* and *sourness* are incompatible.

But the truth or falsity of such reductions of the secondary qualities is not at issue in this work. That is a matter for second philosophy ("speculative cosmology" – Donald Williams, 1953, p. 74) which, under the guidance of science, concerns itself with the question what general sorts of universals there are. Our concern here is with first philosophy, with the general theory of universals. All we are concerned to establish here is the *possibility* of two distinct predicates applying to particulars in virtue of a single universal, or range of universals, which particulars instantiate, but where the first predicate takes the universal (range of universals) as an un-analysed totality while the second predicate articulates the structure of the universal (or range of universals). I note that the possibility was clearly envisaged by Russell (1948, pp. 319–20).

Of course, the chief obstacle to allowing that distinct predicates may apply in virtue of the very same universal is, once again, that obstacle to progress: the Argument from Meaning. If universals are postulated as the meanings of predicates, then semantically distinct predicates must apply in virtue of distinct universals. But any naming predicate and any analysing predicate are semantically distinct. Hence they cannot apply in virtue of the very same universal(s). The response to this argument must, of course, be to reject the identification of universals with meanings.[1]

The case where a naming predicate is replaced by an analysing predicate is of peculiar theoretical interest because the analysing predicate, if really applicable, takes us deeper into the nature of things. But it seems that there can also be cases where distinct naming predicates apply in virtue of the same universal or range of universals. Such a case might arise where a single property was apprehended, but not analysed, by means of two different senses. It might require a theoretical argument to establish that it was the very same property in both cases. The semantical situation would have similarities to that which occurs when Cicero is identified with Tully. Again, there might be distinct analysing predicates applying

---

[1] R. G. Durrant (1970) shows that Moore's famous argument to show that goodness is not identical with pleasure is based upon the same fallacious reasoning.

in virtue of the same universal or range of universals but rendering their structure to different degrees of depth or in different respects. Thus, if 'hot' is a naming predicate, 'temperature' may be an analysing predicate and 'mean kinetic energy of constituent molecules' a predicate which analyses the very same range of properties still more deeply. Since it is logically possible that every universal is infinitely complex, it may be that there is no ultimate analysing predicate.

But predicates may stand to universals or ranges of universals in another way besides "naming" or "analysing" them. This third sort of predicate may be called an "external" predicate.

Consider the predicate 'of the colour Angela prefers'. It is not quite the example we want. It is not a pure predicate because it involves essential reference to a particular. Again, if a thing is of the colour Angela prefers, it is *of a colour*, that is, it is coloured. But 'coloured' is a naming predicate, so the predicate 'of the colour Angela prefers' is *partially* a naming predicate. A better example for our purposes may be the predicate 'brittle'. Suppose that we think of brittleness as an enduring state of the brittle thing. It is controversial whether we have to think of brittleness in this way, but we can obviously assign this meaning to the phonetic-orthographic entity "brittle" if we so choose. With "brittle" so interpreted, 'brittle' becomes an external predicate. It may be unpacked roughly as 'possessing that property (or range of properties) in virtue of which objects (generally) shatter when hit sharply'.

The difference between an external and an analysing predicate is that the former tells us nothing about the internal nature of the universal concerned. We know something about a property if we know only that objects which have the property shatter when sharply hit, but we know nothing of what it is in itself. So 'brittle' is an external predicate.

Like analysing predicates, external predicates are semantically complex. They are structures of semantically simpler predicates. By contrast, naming predicates are not semantically complex. But, although both analysing and external predicates are complex, the complexity of analysing predicates maps (to a greater or lesser extent) the inner complexity of a universal or range of universals; while the external predicates apply in virtue of relations which all and only particulars instantiating the universal(s) in question bear to other particulars of a certain sort.

It follows that the truth-conditions for these three sorts of predicate differ. In the case of naming predicates, it is necessary only that the particulars the predicate applies to instantiate the monadic or polyadic universal(s) in question. In the case of analysing predicates, the particular must not only instantiate the universal(s) but the latter must have the structure spelt out in the analysis. But if external predicates apply, not only must the particulars instantiate the universal(s) in question, but these particulars must stand in certain relations to further particulars of certain sorts, relations which hold in virtue of the original universal(s) instantiated by the original particulars.

As already emphasized, it is the analysing predicates which take us deeper into the nature of the properties themselves. A great deal of scientific advance, therefore, takes the form of passing from naming and from external predicates to analysing ones (representing two sorts of "contingent identification"). The transition from naming to analysing predicate is the case where a totalistically apprehended universal is dissected into constituents. The transition from external to analysing predicate is somewhat different. An example is the identification of brittleness with a certain sort of molecular bonding.

The nature of a predicate may not lie open to casual inspection. Hence logical analysis and/or philosophical argument may be necessary to show that a certain predicate is, say, an external one. I myself hold that mental predicates are external ones (1968, 1973). Mental concepts, I maintain, are concepts of that property or range of properties of a person which play a certain causal role – in particular a role in the causation of that person's behaviour. The causal role involved is exceedingly complex and differs for different mental concepts. I maintain further, as a scientific hypothesis, that the properties in question are purely physical properties of the brain. If all this is correct, then the identification of mental states with states of the brain is a case, even if a peculiarly complex case, of the passage from external to analysing predicates.

To sum up. In the case of referring expressions, philosophers are accustomed to distinguish between their reference and their sense. We recognize that two or more referring expressions may have different senses while having the same reference. We also recognize that referring expressions may refer in different ways. Names, for instance, differ from definite descriptions in their mode of referring. Again, referring expressions may be singular or plural.

We must now recognize that similar distinctions can be drawn in the case of predicates (predicate expressions). We must distinguish between the universal or disjunctive range of universals in virtue of which a predicate applies (these universals correspond to the reference of a referring expression), and the sense of the predicate (its meaning). In the case of a predicate such as 'bewitched' there is no property or range of properties in virtue of which it applies. In this respect 'bewitched' resembles 'Excalibur' or 'The Fountain of Youth'. Predicates with different senses, that is, different predicate-*types*, may apply in virtue of the very same universal or range of universals. Finally, predicates may stand in different ways to the universals or range of universals in virtue of which they apply. They may, for instance, if they are pure predicates, be naming, analysing, or external predicates.

In this Part we have spoken of predicates applying to particulars *in virtue* of properties and relations of those particulars. It may be that a more technical vocabulary is desirable. Confining ourselves to pure open predicates, we might say that a given universal *satisfies* or fails to satisfy the predicate. If a certain monadic universal, P, satisfies a predicate 'F', and if a particular, $a$, has P, then, and only then, 'F' applies to $a$ in virtue of the property, P. The notion of satisfaction here is distinct from, but a close relative of, Tarski's notion of satisfaction.

'Satisfies' will be a two-place predicate. The satisfaction of predicates by universals may or may not be a genuine relation. The investigation of this semantic predicate, how in detail a predicate stands to a universal when the latter satisfies the former, could only be a major research project. But the introduction of a term may serve to focus our minds on the problem.

# 18

## *Properties*

In the previous Part various important conclusions in the theory of universals were arrived at. But these conclusions were reached in the course of examining the different ways in which predicates stand to universals. The next two chapters attempt to advance the theory of universals more directly. This chapter treats of properties, the next of relations. I shall, however, defer the discussion of *relational* properties until ch. 19.

### 1 *Are all monadic universals properties?*

Every property is a monadic universal. But is every monadic universal a property? It has been tacitly assumed in the course of the argument so far that there are no other sorts of monadic universal besides properties. This assumption now requires defence.

Two other types of monadic universal have been proposed. First, there are reflexive relations, where a particular is related to itself. This notion will be criticized in the next chapter, where it will be argued that all relations are polyadic, holding between at least two particulars. Second, there are what may be called "substantival" universals. They form the subject of the present section.

*Being gold* has quite a good claim to be a monadic universal. But it sounds strange to say that it is a property. *Being gold* is being a certain sort of stuff. *Being an electron* has at least equal claim to be a monadic universal. It sounds equally strange to say that it is a property. *Being an electron* is being a certain sort of thing.

I intend to contrast *being an electron* and *being gold* here. In the phrase introduced in ch. 11 § iv, *being an electron* is a "particularizing" universal, one which permits its instances to be numbered. We know as a matter of science that *being gold* is *being so many atoms of gold.* If this fact is taken into consideration, then the desired contrast between these two (putative) monadic universals is destroyed. For the sake of examples, however, the reader is asked to abstract from this scientific knowledge here.

Although there is a contrast between sorts of stuff and sorts of thing, *prima facie* neither are properties. If it can be shown further that it is impossible to give a reductive account of stuffs and sorts of things in terms of their properties, then it will be necessary to admit a second category of monadic universal alongside properties. Universals of this second category may be called *irreducibly substantival universals*, and the doctrine that there are such universals *Essentialist Realism*. The view is to be found in Aristotle, and, under his influence, the Scholastics. For contemporary attempts to work out versions of Essentialist Realism see M. H. Thompson (1953) and M. J. Loux (1974 and 1976). Loux concerns himself solely with *particularizing* substantival universals.

It cannot be denied that particulars have properties. Essentialist Realism is therefore a doctrine that associated with each (true) particular is a super-universal, in some way standing behind, enfolding and explaining the mere properties. It is traditional for such a theory to distinguish between essential and accidental properties, the latter standing in much more contingent and loose relationship to the substantival universal than the former.

I do not know how to refute, but I find two difficulties in, the doctrine(s) of Essentialist Realism.

First, there is an argument from simplicity. Suppose that a particular has all the properties which are required for something to be gold or for something to be an electron. Will it not be gold or be an electron? Why postulate some further universal which it must exemplify in order to be gold or an electron? It is true that there may be in addition nomic connections between these properties which bind the properties up into a unity. (It will be argued in ch. 24 that such nomic connections are relations between the properties.) But given such a unified bunch of properties (itself a property according to the doctrine of conjunctive universals put forward in ch. 15), what need of a further unifying universal? It may be conceded that actually to say of something that it has all the properties of gold is normally to hint that the thing is not, or may not be, gold. But there seems to be no reason to take this usage to be a significant pointer to the ontology of the situation.

Second, there is an argument from symmetry. The theory being put forward in this book follows Peirce, William James and Russell in giving full and ungrudging recognition to polyadic universals, that is, to relations. Aristotle, by contrast, said of relations in the *Metaphysics* that they are "least of all things a kind of entity or substance" (1088a 22). But once relations are recognized as perfectly good universals alongside monadic universals, it seems natural to take the true monadic universals to be properties. It is they that are the natural siblings to relations. Donald Williams has spoken of a "relation-rope", the totality of relations which hold between two particulars (1963, p. 604). But Williams does not suggest, and there seems no reason to hold, that the relation-rope is anything more than the conjunction of all the relations involved.

For these two reasons, then, I propose that we should try to account for substantival universals in terms of properties.

The doctrine of Essentialist Realism is closely bound up with the view that there are certain ways, and these ways only, of dividing the world up into particulars. A man, or in a more scientifically-oriented version of the theory, an electron, may be a true particular, but a portion of one man plus a portion of another, or a portion of one electron plus a portion of another, is not a true particular. By contrast, if Essentialist Realism is rejected, it would seem that any collection of particulars or parts of particulars, scattered or not in space and in time, constitutes a particular. Any part of a particular is a particular. Any compound of particulars is a particular, though some particulars will lack that nomic unity which "natural" particulars have. It may then be pointed out that this doctrine, taken together with the doctrine of universals defended in this book, introduces a queer asymmetry into the theory of particulars and universals. We have put sharp limitations on what constitutes a genuine universal, a one genuinely capable of running through many particulars. But in the case of particulars, it appears, we have embraced a position of complete tolerance.

I wish now to suggest that there is a limitation, if only a theoretical one, upon the compounding of particulars to give a further particular. All the particulars which we have any reason to postulate are related to each other in a single space-time. This is the doctrine of Naturalism (see ch. 12). *As a result*, the compounding of them yields further particulars. But consider two particulars belonging to two distinct space-times. They would lack spatio-temporal relations to each other, and might lack any other genuine relations. (No doubt it will always be possible to manufacture some two-place predicate applying to them both. But that, of course, does not entail the existence of a real relation.) Two such particulars, I suggest, would not make up the proper parts of a particular.

Furthermore, although Essentialist Realism has been rejected, it does seem that it has an element of truth. We might call the truth involved the *Principle of Particularization.* It is the truth that, for each particular, there exists at least one monadic universal which makes that particular just one, and not more than one, instance of a certain sort. Such a universal will be a "particularizing" universal, making that particular *one* of a kind. Without such a universal, the particular is not restricted to certain definite bounds, it is not "signed to a certain quantity", we do not have a "substance", we do not have *a* particular.

Suppose, then, that the Principle of Particularization be accepted, but at the same time, unlike traditional Essentialist Realism, we also accept the indefinite dividing and compounding of particulars, at least in the same space-time. What will the particularizing universals be? I can see nothing which is *always* available except the *spatio-temporal pattern* possessed by the total or spatio-temporal position of the particular involved. Consider an ordinary object with a beginning and an end. The space-time worm will have definite dimensions and definite spatio-temporal structure which other particulars can also possess. Here is a property which is a particularizing universal, perhaps the only particularizing universal which the particular has. The universal need not "divide its instantiations" in the full-blooded way that, say, *being an electron* yields a number of discrete electrons. By contrast, *having a certain spatio-temporal pattern* will be instantiated in overlapping, partially identical, particulars. In the terminology introduced in ch. 11 § IV, it is only a *weakly* particularizing universal. But the universal will yield an unambiguous answer to the question whether a certain particular is or is not *one* instance of that universal. (Contrast *being of a certain shade of red.*)

The hypothesis may be advanced further that, as a matter of fact, all particularizing universals involve as constituent parts, such particularizing universals of spatio-temporal pattern, and, lacking such parts, would not be particularizing universals. This would be compatible with the view that such spatio-temporal patterns are not fundamental, but rather scientifically analysable, features of reality.

Turning back now from these high matters, we may note that the ontological doctrine that an account can be given of substantival universals purely in terms of the *properties* of particulars must not be thought to commit us to any particular semantic doctrines. *Being gold* and *being an electron* are instances of natural kinds, the first being a kind of stuff, the second a kind of thing. As Putnam (1970b) indicates, it is very important to distinguish sharply between the ontology of natural kinds and the semantics of natural-kind words. It is traditional semantic doctrine that natural-kind words apply to particulars in virtue of a certain set of properties, known to the user of the word, which are necessary and sufficient to make the object a thing of that kind. This semantic doctrine appears to be false. But its falsity does not affect the ontological claim that an account can be given of the nature of natural kinds purely in terms of their properties.

Consider a typical case of the application of the predicate 'crimson'. Objects having the property, crimson (or, perhaps better, having one of the disjunctive range of properties covered by that predicate) act upon our sense-organs. They act in virtue of *the crimsonness of the object*. As a result of this causal action we correctly apply the predicate 'crimson'. Properties and predicates are lined up in a neat and simple way.

It is this rather simple model which we try to apply to natural kinds like gold. We assume that there are certain gold-making properties, we recognize them, and then apply the predicate 'gold'. But what are the properties? It seems difficult to say. Different people use different tests to tell that something is gold. As Putnam points out, most people simply take the word of experts.

But it does not follow from the fact that the semantics of 'gold' is quite different from, and much harder to elucidate than, the semantics of 'crimson', that *being gold* is not a (complex) property. Of course, there may be scientific reasons for thinking that *being gold* is not really a universal at all, but simply a (close-knit) family of universals. But we are agreeing to ignore that latter possibility.

However, there may be one difference between the concept of a natural kind and the concept of an (ordinary) property which is not covered simply by treating the natural kind as a much more complex property. In ch. 11 § v, we distinguished between "abstract" and "concrete" particulars. Distinct abstract particulars can occupy exactly the same place at the same time (the "visual cube" and the "tactual cube"). This is not so for concrete particulars (the common-sense cube). Now, given a concrete particular made up of two or more abstract particulars, a property like *being crimson* might be a property both of one of the abstract particulars (the "visual cube") and the concrete particular (the cube). But it seems that to be a piece of gold, the particular can *only* be a concrete particular. Our concept of gold is such that if there is a piece of gold at a certain place and time, then there can be nothing else at exactly that place and time.

This, I think, at least partially justifies the special link which the Aristotelian tradition saw between substantival universals such as *being gold* and *being an electron* and individuation. If a particular is crimson, and at a certain place and time, it is not thereby determined what particular it is, for there can be a plurality of (abstract) particulars at that place and time. But if a thing is gold or is an electron, and is at a certain place and time, the individual involved is fixed.

A natural kind, then, is a certain sort of *concrete* particular. How can we characterize it further? If we consider portions of gold, then many of the properties of such portions, such as shape, size and many relational properties, will vary independently from portion to portion. But there will be a great many of the properties of such portions which do not vary much, or, where they do vary, vary along a relatively narrow range. It is these *relatively invariable* properties (colour, ductility, etc.) which are, for the expert at least, diagnostic. They tell him that the substance is, almost certainly, gold. They correspond roughly to what Locke would have called the *nominal essence* of gold. There will be various sorts of nomic connection between these properties.

The notion of a nomically united cluster of diagnostic properties does not, however, exhaust the notion of a natural kind. It is a more theoretical concept than that. Behind the set of "surface" properties there is a set of more deeply hidden properties: the *real essence* of the natural kind. If the natural kind is to be a genuine monadic universal, then this real essence will have to be identical in every instance of the kind. But even if such identity is lacking, the set of properties constituting the real essence will constitute a closer unity than the set constituting the diagnostic properties (the nominal essence).

It is from the real essence that the nominal essence flows. The deeply hidden, but central, properties *nomically necessitate* that, in various standard or special circumstances, the object has the diagnostic properties.

This Lockean-inspired sketch of the notion of a natural kind is no doubt somewhat jejune. I have not been able to carry it any further. But I think it indicates that it is at least perfectly possible to give an account of "substantival" universals purely in terms of properties. We have still to consider the question whether there are any reflexive relations. But substantival universals, at least, seem to pose no threat to the thesis that all monadic universals are properties.

## 11 *Simple and complex properties*

It is not a necessary truth that there are complex properties, but it is an undeniable fact. It is another undeniable fact that there are properties which appear to us to be simple. But it is an open question whether or not there are any properties which actually are simple. If the question is ever decided, it will not be decided by the *a priori* methods of philosophy.

If a property is complex, then it has parts. These parts are properties and/or relations. We will call them the *constituents* of the complex property. A complex property may or may not have *ultimate* constituents, i.e. simple properties and simple relations.

If a complex property has ultimate constituents, then these constituents may be finite in number. But it seems possible also that a complex property might have ultimate constituents, yet there be an infinite number of these ultimates. If this is really possible, then we must distinguish two sorts of infinite complexity which properties might have. First, the infinitely complex property might be a complex of simple constituents, but simples of which there are an infinite number. Second, the infinitely complex property might dissolve *ad infinitum* into constituents which themselves lacked simple constituents, either a finite or an infinite number. The two cases may be compared to two views of the nature of extensions and durations. According to one view, they are infinite collections of simple points and instants. According to another view, they contain no simple constituents, even "at infinity". In the case of properties, at least, it seems that "infinite complexity" might take either form.

Of course, a complex property might be resolvable in part into ultimate constituents while containing other constituents not so resolvable. It is logically possible, for instance, that properties dissolve for ever into things-having-certain-properties-in-certain-relations, where the properties contain no simple properties, even an infinity of simple properties, but the relations do terminate in simple relations.

### III *Unstructural and structural properties*

Having drawn the distinction between simple and complex properties, we may draw the distinction between unstructural and structural properties. Again it is the case that, while we know that there are structural properties, it is logically and epistemically possible that there are no unstructural properties.

Before drawing this distinction it is required that we first draw the old distinction between *homoeomerous* and *anomoeomerous* properties, a distinction going back as far as Anaxagoras, though he appears to have applied it to stuffs rather than properties. A property is homoeomerous if and only if for all particulars, $x$, which have that property, then for all *parts y* of $x$, $y$ also has that property. If a property is not homoeomerous, then it is anomoeomerous.

Here are some *prima facie* examples of homoeomerous properties: *having mass, having length, being a certain shade of blue* (shade C), *having the properties of gold*. But the examples are suspect. First, there are reasons to think that *having mass* and *having length* are not properties but disjunctive (although homogeneous) ranges of properties.[1] (This matter is to be discussed in ch. 22.) There may well be such properties as *having a mass of one kilogram exactly* or *being one metre long exactly*. But these are anomoeomerous properties. The proper parts of a thing of mass one kilogram do not have the mass of one kilogram. Second, *being a certain shade C of blue*, or *having the properties of gold*, though they may be properties, are very likely not homoeomerous. To the mere look and appearance they are homoeomerous. They are "homoeomerous at the macroscopic level". But get down to wave-lengths and atoms, and it appears that they are anomoeomerous. However, since there may be no genuinely

---

[1] It might still be said that the *predicates* 'having mass' and 'having length' are "homoeomerously applicable predicates". (Goodman calls them "dissective" predicates – 1966, p. 53.) For where the predicates are applicable to a particular they are also applicable (it is quite plausible to say) to any part of that particular. But, of course, that does not prove that homoeomerous *properties* are involved.

homoeomerous properties, we can pretend here that they are examples of homoeomerous properties.

Homoeomerous properties may be simple or they may be complex. A determinate shade of blue has a superficial claim to be simple as well as being homoeomerous. However, it is not hard to discover reasons for thinking that it must be complex even without appealing to scientific data. In the case of gold, the very phrase 'having the properties of gold' shows that we are dealing with a complex property. It may be infinitely complex; gold may have an inexhaustible nature. Our *concept* of gold may be a very inadequate concept indeed, giving us a quite superficial grip on this nature (see § 1).

The notion of a *structural* property may now be introduced. It is a species of anomoeomerous property. A property, S, is structural if and only if proper parts of particulars having S have some property or properties, T . . . not identical with S, and this state of affairs is, in part at least, constitutive of S. It will be seen that a structural property must be complex.

It might be wondered whether structural properties are not simply identical with anomoeomerous properties. The difficulty with this suggestion is that it seems possible that particulars might have *over-all* or *emergent* properties which characterized no proper parts of the particular, and so were anomoeomerous, but which were distinct from any property-structure possessed by the particulars having the emergent property. For instance, a quantity of homoeomerous stuff having certain definite dimensions might be further characterized by such an emergent property. Unlike a structural property, such a property could be simple, although it could also be complex (by being conjunctive). Characteristically, reductionists do not believe in the existence of properties of this sort, and I myself think that there are good methodological and scientific reasons for being sceptical about claims that such properties exist. But I cannot see that their existence can be ruled out *a priori*.

Structural properties, however, are anomoeomerous properties which are not of this sort. It will be noted that the concept of *a state of affairs* was used in the definition of structural property. Consider the structural property of *being (just) two electrons*, a property possessed by all two-member collections of electrons. We cannot say that this property involves the same universal, *being an electron*, taken twice over, because a universal is one, not many. We can only say that the more complex universal involves the notion of two particulars of a certain sort, two instances of the same universal state of affairs.

*Being (just) two electrons* is not merely a structural property, but it is a *particularizing* property. Indeed, it is a *strongly* particularizing property. (For the notions, see § 1, and ch. 11 § iv.) This raises the question whether *every* structural property is a particularizing property. I am inclined to think that it must be, although it is clear that it need not be a *strongly* particularizing property. In the definition of structural property I introduced the notion of a property, T, possessed by particulars which are proper parts of the particulars which have the structural property. I think that T, also, must be a particularizing property. But I do not know how to prove these contentions.

At the end of ch. 15 § 11, attention was called to the *Conjunction Principle*, the principle that, if a universal is complex, its constituents, which are also universals, instantiate the very same particulars which the complex universal instantiates. It was pointed out that there is no reason to accept the Principle. It holds for conjunctive properties but only for conjunctive properties. It is structural properties which have suffered because of the Principle. The Principle is an obstacle to seeing that the universals involved in structural properties are just as much parts of the structural properties as the conjuncts are parts of conjunctive universals.

## iv *Two types of structural property*

Structural properties may or may not involve certain relations among the parts of the particulars having the properties. Consider the putative property, *being one kilogram in mass exactly*. This is a structural property. The proper parts of one-kilogram particulars are not one-kilogram particulars. These parts, individually weighing less than one kilogram, together make up an object of mass one kilogram. But no particular *relations* between these parts seem involved in the object having this property. For instance, the parts may be scattered parts. Compare this with *being a hydrogen atom* or *being a certain tartan pattern*. Not every particular which contains the essential constituents of a hydrogen atom is, or even contains, a hydrogen atom. To be a hydrogen atom, a particular must include an electron and a proton. But, more than this, the electron and proton must stand *in certain relations*. The particular made up of an electron in atom A and a proton in atom B is not a hydrogen atom. To be a token of a certain tartan pattern, it is necessary that a particular include certain sorts of constituents (yellow stripes, etc.). But it is further necessary that the constituents be arranged in a certain way.

We will say of the latter type of structural property that it is a *relationally* structural property. It includes relations among its parts. Properties like *being one kilogram in mass* will be said to be *non-relationally* structural properties.

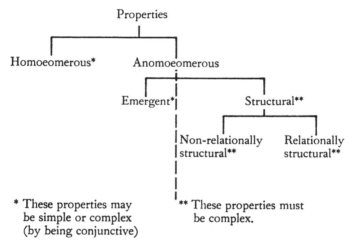

Fig. 2

We may sum up the classification of properties proposed in this chapter in fig. 2. It should be noted that the classification is really a classification of *possible* properties, because there may in fact be no properties of the sort listed on the left-hand side of the dotted line.

### v *Numbers and properties*

Could number be a property of particulars? Frege (1884, § 22) and others developed an argument, now widely used, to show that number is not such a property. The argument is that a particular has no definite number until it has been brought under some concept. Consider the particular which is the aggregate of the Fs. Given a suitable concept, it may have the number nought, one, two . . .

I believe that we ought to be suspicious of this argument. It amounts to saying that numbers are not properties of particulars because particulars have indefinitely many numbers. Might not the correct reaction be to say that the particulars have *all* these numbers as properties?

Consider some ordinary particular, such as this page. It may be said to be *two-parted*. That is to say, there exists an *x* and there exists a *y*, wholly distinct from *x*, such that the aggregate of *x* and *y* constitutes the particular which is the page. In the case of the page the two parts will, in general, be physically separable. But such physical separability is not part of the notion of *being two-parted*. It is much more general than that. Is this not a *property* of the page? It seems to be something which could be identical in different particulars. I suggest that it is a structural though not a relationally structural property of the page. It is also a formal property, because it can be analysed purely in terms of formal, or topic-neutral, notions. Taking this view does have the consequence that anything which has parts has something genuinely in common with anything else which has parts. But I see no reason to reject this consequence.

The page is, of course, *three-parted, four-parted* . . . perhaps *infinitely-parted*. I suggest that these are all structural properties of the page. These properties will stand to each other as parts to wholes. If something is four-parted, then it is entailed that it is three-parted. This is explained by saying that the property, *being four-parted*, contains as a proper part the property, *being three-parted*.

As already remarked, the page may have an infinity of these structural properties. But a particular which is absolutely indivisible, if there are any such, would have none of these properties. (Remember, also, that the lack of a property is not a property.) A particular which was nothing more than two absolutely indivisible particulars would have the property, *being two-parted*, but no other of these structural properties.

The question now arises whether these structural properties can be identified with the numbers. It is clear that they cannot. In the first place, the numbers 0 and 1 are not provided for. In the second place, suppose that as a matter of fact, there is an upper limit to the complexity of the universe. Given the Principle of Instantiation, then, if the numbers were identical with these structural properties, the numbers would stop when that point of complexity had been reached. This seems absurd.

This second difficulty can be met by modifying the thesis that the numbers are identical with the properties, *being two-parted, being three-parted,* etc. Instead, it can be suggested that the numbers are identical with the *logically possible* set of properties, *being two-parted, being three-parted,* etc. The universe may or may not have an infinite number of parts. But it is logically possible that it has an infinite number of parts, where the phrase "infinite number" covers all the orders of infinity. To talk about the "existence" of numbers would be simply to talk about the logical possibility of the corresponding formal properties. This seems a reasonably plausible view of mathematical existence.

The formal structural properties themselves would remain as the foundation in things which permits numerical predicates to be applied to the things.

Of course, in order to carry this view through it would be necessary to produce a satisfactory theory of logical possibility within the ontological framework adopted in this work. In particular, an account of logical possibility is required which makes no appeal to an ontology of possible worlds. As indicated at the end of ch. 15 § III, I am hopeful that this can be done, by producing a semantic or *de dicto* theory of logical possibility, although I am far from clear about the details.

But we are still left with the problem of the numbers 0 and 1. How can they be structural properties of particulars, actual or possible?

It is here that we must turn back to something a little nearer a traditional account of number. Suppose it to be the case that there are three, and only three, apples in the room. The aggregate of these apples is a particular. This particular has an indefinite number of parts, perhaps an infinite number. But this particular has three and only three parts such that the predicate 'an apple' applies to them. It is highly unlikely that 'an apple' is a strictly universal predicate, applying in virtue of a single monadic universal. All the same, the predicate will apply in virtue of certain properties (which may be different in the case of each of the three apples) which the three parts of the aggregate have. There is therefore *some* structural property of the aggregate, involving three distinct parts which together make up the aggregate. It is this structural property, involving three parts, each with certain apple-making properties, which makes it true that the aggregate is an instance of three apples. It is in virtue of this property, in other words, that the predicate 'three apples' applies to this particular. Such a property is more complex than the formal property, *being three-parted*. It is a matter of the aggregate having three parts, but three parts such that each of them has properties which make that part exactly one apple. Such complex structural properties will often be of much greater interest than the very abstract, formal, properties originally described.

The number 1 and the number 0 are now seen to be introduced in connection with these more complex properties. To say that something is one-parted, that it is one, is to say nothing at all.[1] But a particular can have properties which make it, not an aggregate of three apples, but simply *an apple*. It is convenient, therefore, to have the number 1 to apply to this limiting case of those various structural properties which make a particular an aggregate of apples.

The number 0 is a device introduced to deal with a still more extreme case. To say that there is no apple in the room is to say of each particular in the room that it is not an apple. There is no property of *not being an apple*, there are simply the particulars in the room with whatever (positive) properties they happen to have. But by means of the numbers 1 and 0 all the possibilities are covered. If 'an apple' applies to a plurality of particulars in the room, some numeral greater than '1' is applicable. If the predicate has application, but not to a plurality of particulars, the numeral '1' can be used. If neither of these things obtains, then the numeral '0' is used. Something makes it true that there are no apples in the room, but this truth-maker is simply the contents of the room with their (positive) properties.

It is often said that number is a property of *classes*. But if a class is taken *distributively* (that is, if the class-expression is used as a plural referring expression – see ch. 4 § 1), then it does not seem to be the case that number attaches to the class. Number attaches not to the class as many, but to the class as one, that is, it attaches to the *aggregate* of the members. But it attaches to the aggregate taken not just as a heap, but taken as exemplifying a certain (strongly) particularizing property or properties. The particularizing property or properties divide the aggregate into *a certain number of parts*.

---

[1] Owens (1961), writing about the doctrine of St. Thomas, says: "Unity is a negative aspect. Once the existence is there, no further positive characteristic is required to make a thing one. Unity follows as a negation of division, once a thing exists" (p. 251). I would only add that all characteristics are positive.

# 19
## *Relations*

This century has seen great advances in the topic of the logic of relations. Unfortunately, advances in the philosophy of relations have not been comparable. In the early decades the important question of internal and external relations attracted a good deal of attention. But with the decline in influence of the Absolute Idealists, who held that the conception of an internal is truer than that of an external relation, the dispute died away.

Even those philosophers who have exhibited a fairly firm grip of the notion of property have often been puzzled by relations. Plato betrays his perplexity in many passages. As already mentioned, Aristotle said of relations that they were "least of all things a kind of entity or substance" (1088a 22).[1] Locke asserted that relations were not contained in "the real existence of things" but were "something extraneous and superinduced" (II, 8). Leibniz's strictures on relations are well known. Even Russell, whose contribution to the topic of relations is so great, can be found saying in 1911 that:

> General qualities, such as whiteness . . . may be said to be in many places at once

yet also remarking:

> Relations, obviously, do not exist anywhere in space. (p. 3)

For us, however, properties are one-particulared or monadic universals, while relations are two-, three-, *n*-particulared, that is dyadic, triadic, *n*-adic universals. Properties are just the simplest case of universals. This truth was eventually grasped by Russell, though he sometimes put the point unnecessarily paradoxically by

---

[1] Since I have several times described my position on universals as "Aristotelian", it may be useful to indicate my attitude to various features of Aristotle's own theory. What I accept is his Immanent Realism, an Immanent Realism which can be plausibly interpreted as *non-relational* (see ch. 10). But I reject (1) the special position he accords to monadic as opposed to polyadic universals; (2) his doctrine of irreducibly substantial universals which determine the true essence of certain particulars and make them *the* particulars. It goes without saying that an *a posteriori* Realism is not committed to the particular universals which Aristotle recognizes.

describing properties as "monadic relations" (1918, p. 199; 1940, p. 94). This latter phrase should surely be reserved for cases, if there are any, of reflexive relations.

What is more complex is more difficult for the intellect to grasp. This simple reason, I suggest, explains why, in a field of study as peculiarly difficult as ontology, relations, by comparison with properties, have been neglected or have been so confusingly treated. At the same time, it suggests that the topic of relations may prove a peculiarly rewarding one for the theory of universals as a whole. For it may be expected that important classifications and distinctions which can be made at the level of polyadic universals will vanish, or become merely notional, in the limiting monadic case. What is said in this chapter, however, may not do very much to meet sanguine expectation. I suspect that it only scratches the surface.

## 1 *Relations and instantiation*

The Principle of Instantiation for properties asserts that, for each property, P, there exists (not necessarily now) a particular, $x$, such that P$x$. Platonism about properties is the denial of this principle. The familiar assertion that relations must have terms is simply the Principle applied to relations. Its denial seems particularly strange with respect to relations. An entity which depends for its existence upon at least two other entities is perhaps more obviously a dependent thing than one which only depends upon one. The more obvious dependence may also help to explain why Aristotle and others accorded relations a low degree of reality.

However, the fact that relations relate two or more particulars opens up a "possibility" not present in the case of properties: that of merely partial instantiation. It might be maintained that there can be $n$-place relations, where only $m$ "places" are filled by particulars, $m$ being greater than o but less than $n$. Nor need we look far for *prima facie* cases. The Apostles expected the Second Coming. The Apostles are perfectly good particulars, but the Second Coming is (I assume) a myth. So, it may be argued, in this as in many other 'intentional' contexts, a relation, in this case the relation of *expecting*, is partially instantiated only.

The traditional Anglo-Saxon interpretation of Meinong is that, faced with such cases, he tries to reinstate the Principle of Instantiation by providing the mythical Second Coming with some sort of being. The cost is an extraordinary ontology. However, Grossmann (1974) argues that Meinong holds that the relation has a second term but one which has no sort of being. In effect, then, Meinong denies the Principle of Instantiation for the second term of the relation. The difficulty then is to distinguish between various false expectations that the Apostles may have had. For "different nothings" would all seem to be "the same thing", *viz.* nothing at all.

The obvious solution of the difficulty, however, is to deny that *expecting* is a two-place universal. This reminds us that the sharp distinction between predicates and universals and their failure to correlate in any simple way, so important in the cases of properties, must be generalized and carried through to the case of relations. 'Expects' is certainly a two-place predicate. But there need not be a dyadic relation of *expecting*. Instead, we can say that 'expecting the Second Coming' is a complex one-place predicate, applying to the Apostles in virtue of certain complex properties or ranges of complex properties which they instantiate. (These properties may well include relational properties, but not, of course, relational properties involving relations to the Second Coming!) Just what these properties are is a very difficult question to answer, involving all sorts of problems of philosophical analysis and scientific identification which cannot be entered upon here. (I should say that it is a matter of a certain complex structuring of the Apostles' brains.) But such a solution, however much toil it may mean in other fields, seems clearly preferable to giving up the Principle of Instantiation (or inflating our ontology with objects of expectation).

Before concluding this section, it may be noted that the distinction between simple and complex applies as much to relations as to properties. Again, it seems that a distinction between homoeomerous and anomoeomerous can also be drawn in the case of relations. If, for all $x$ and for all $y$ such that $x$ has R to $y$, any part of $x$ also has R to any part of $y$, then R may be said to be a homoeomerous relation. If a relation is not homoeomerous it is anomoeomerous. However, although it is relatively easy to find many-place *predicates* which are "homoeomerous in their application", there can be few, if any, homoeomerous polyadic universals.

As Keith Campbell has pointed out to me, the greater complication in the case of relations opens up further possibilities of classification absent in the case of properties. Suppose, for instance, that *being wholly enclosed by* is a genuine dyadic universal. A box may wholly enclose the contents of the box. This supposed relation is not, in Campbell's term, "left" homoeomerous because it is not true that every part of an enclosing box encloses the contents of the box. But it is "right" homoeomerous, because every part of the contents of a box is enclosed by the box.

## II *Relational properties*

The predicate-type 'revolves around the sun' applies to all the planets of our solar system. But there is no property of *revolving around the sun*, for the predicate involves essential reference to a particular: the sun. The predicate is not a *pure* predicate. If for no other reason, then, it is not a property-predicate. In general, if $a$ and $b$ are particulars, and if $a$ has R to $b$, then 'Rb' and 'R̆a' apply to $a$ and $b$ respectively but are not property-predicates.

But, of course, to reject 'revolves around the sun' as property-predicate is to invite consideration of *pure* predicates such as 'revolves around a star' or, for that matter, 'revolves around something'. May there not be relational properties of *revolving around a star* and *revolving around something*; or at least may there not be a range of relational properties in virtue of which the pure predicates 'revolves around a star' and 'revolves around something' apply?

It seems that we must admit relational properties. Suppose R to be a relation, F a property, and suppose that there is at least one particular which has R to a particular with property, F. *Having R to something with property, F,* would seem to be something identical which an indefinite number of particulars could have, particulars at any place or time. So it is a genuine relational property, and the corresponding predicate is a species of property-predicate.

But although it seems that we must admit relational properties, the admission is of little ontological importance. For we can give a reductive account of relational properties in terms of non-relational properties and relations.

Suppose that the predicate 'revolves around a star' applies to a particular, $a$. We can give an account of the situation by saying that there exists a particular, $x$, such that $x$ is a star and that $a$ revolves around $x$. This analysis dispenses with the predicate 'revolves around a star' in favour of the one-place predicate 'being a star' and the two-place predicate 'revolves around'. The first predicate would appear to apply in virtue of *non-relational* properties of $x$, the second in virtue of *relations* holding between $a$ and $x$. This analysis, of course, is the one which would be automatically adopted by contemporary logicians. If it is correct, then relational properties, although real, are not anything over and above the non-relational properties and the relations of particulars.

But here perhaps we should be a little careful. Given (a) the relations in which a particular stands to other particulars; and (b) the non-relational properties of these other particulars; then the relational properties of the original particular are given. This shows that we *need* not postulate relations, non-relational properties and, in addition, relational properties. But this does not prove that we should recognize non-relational properties and relations as fundamental. Suppose, instead, that we started with non-relational and relational properties. We would not then need relations in addition. So we require some reason for deciding between these two schemes.

One simple argument in favour of admitting relations as fundamental is this. It is clear that relational properties are complex properties. What are their parts? Obviously, they can only be *relations* and *non-relational properties*. (These parts are not properties of the particular which has the relational property, but they are parts of that relational property nevertheless.) But if relational properties require relations as constituents, then we cannot give an account of relations in terms of relational properties.

Relational properties are an (analysable) species of monadic universal, but the analysis involves a relation, that is, a polyadic universal, holding between the particular which has the relational property and a further particular or particulars. Reasons of symmetry would lead us to expect that two, three or $n$ particulars instantiate universals which are otherwise formally similar to relational *properties*. This seems to be the case. Two slices of bread, for instance, may be said to *sandwich a piece of ham*. *Sandwiching a piece of ham* is utterly unlikely to be a genuine universal, but here it can be taken to be a dyadic universal for the sake of an example. If the slices of bread are each taken by themselves, then they do not sandwich a piece of ham. *Sandwiching a piece of ham* is not a relational property of either slice. Rather, the two slices of bread and the piece of ham enter into a triadic relation and, as a logical consequence, the two slices of bread exemplify a dyadic universal. This universal seems to be the dyadic companion to the monadic notion of a relational property. It might be called a "relational dyadic universal". And although *sandwiching a piece of ham* is not a satisfactory example of a universal, 'sandwiching a piece of ham' is a genuine (pure) relationally dyadic predicate.

It appears, then, that the phenomenon of a relational property can be duplicated for dyadic and *n*-adic cases. The universals involved in both the monadic and the polyadic cases may be perfectly genuine. But, because they are analysable, they involve no addition to our ontology.

## III *Relational Realism*

We admit non-relational properties, i.e. monadic universals (henceforward usually termed "properties"). We also admit relations, i.e. polyadic universals. But do we admit too much? In particular, should we admit irreducibly monadic universals? It can hardly be denied that particulars have properties. But is it possible to maintain that every property is analysable without remainder in terms of relations?

It is clear in the first place that *some* properties can be analysed in terms of further properties together with relations. These are the properties which in the previous chapter were called "relationally structural" properties. Suppose, for instance, that *a* is composed of wholly distinct parts, *b* and *c*, and that *b* has property F and *c* has property G. *b* and *c* stand in the relation R. It will then be a relationally structural property of *a* that it is made up of a part which is F having R to the remainder of *a*, a remainder having the property G. (Conversely, wherever particulars of a certain sort are related, we can take the particulars as a single particular, a particular having a relationally structural property or properties determined by the properties and mutual relations of the original particulars.)

The thesis that every property is analysable without remainder in terms of relations can now be put in the form: *every property is a relationally structural property*. Is this, or could this be, true?

If this thesis is to be true, then, in the example just given, the properties F and G must themselves be relationally structural properties. Further properties will then be required, which must in turn dissolve. There are then two *prima facie* possibilities open. The first is that this dissolution of properties into relational structures continues *ad infinitum*. The second is that at some point in the analysis of the properties, we reach relationally structural properties which involve particulars which stand in certain relations to each other but lack any (non-relational) properties. Given that either of these scenarios is possible, then we can see how every monadic universal could be analysed in terms of polyadic universals.

C. S. Peirce was a Realist about universals, sometimes describing himself as a Scholastic Realist. But, unlike the Scholastics, he held that all universals were relations. He is therefore described by W. B. Gallie as a Relational Realist (1952, ch. 6). Peirce appears to have been influenced on this matter by F. E. Abbot (1886) who, interestingly, described his own position on universals as *scientific* Realism. Abbot is sketchy, and sometimes, confusingly, speaks of resemblances when it seems that he should be speaking of relations, but he appears to be a Relational Realist. He coined the phrase *universalia inter res* to describe his position, a tag which deserves resurrection.

Peirce seems to have thought that there cannot be monadic universals. His argument appears to have been this. He grasped very thoroughly the point argued for in ch. 16 § 1, that if different properties are to be recognized as different, then it is necessary that they each bestow different powers upon the particulars whose properties they are. He saw further that different powers can only be recognized to be different if they actually give rise to different manifestations. The recognition of different properties as different thus depends upon the relations which the particulars having the properties have to further particulars. Peirce, then, would have accepted, and accepted enthusiastically, Scotus' dictum:

*sed forma non cognoscitur nisi ex operationibus.*

But at this point Peirce makes a move quite foreign to the thought of Scotus. In positivistic or phenomenalistic style, he *identifies* the property with those effects wrought by particulars which the property is responsible for. Thus he reaches his Relational Realism.

There appear to be at least two difficulties in Peirce's position. First, to give an account of properties in terms of effects arouses suspicion of circularity in his analysis. For what can these effects be but effects of a certain *sort*, and how is the notion of sort to be explicated except by appeal to the notion of property? Second, how do relations escape the same positivist dialectic to which Peirce exposes properties? How can we recognize that *a* stands in R to *b* unless this state of affairs has its effect upon the world, and ultimately upon our mind? If alternatively the state of affairs can be recognized without further ado, why can it not also be recognized directly that *a* has the property F? For these two reasons, I reject Peirce's arguments for his Relational Realism.

The correct position I take to be this. While it is not *necessary* (as Peirce seems to maintain) that all properties dissolve into relations, so that all monadic universals are analysed in terms of polyadic ones, it is *possible* that this is the case. Furthermore, I think that the possibility is an epistemic one. It is compatible with everything which at present we know or can rationally conjecture. But the hypothesis of Relational Realism seems in no better epistemic shape than the rival hypothesis that there are irreducibly monadic universals.

We may now return to the two (*prima facie*) possible ways in which a Relational Realism may be developed. The second of these ways is the hypothesis that we finally reach ultimate particulars. These particulars have relations to each other, but lack any (non-relational) properties, even relationally structural properties. Although completely lacking in any internal nature, such particulars will not be "bare particulars". For they would instantiate universals, *viz.* relations. They would simply fail to instantiate any monadic universals. All particulars which in any way differed or agreed in non-relational properties, would have to be compound particulars made up of these fundamental particulars related in various ways. This may be Wittgenstein's view in the *Tractatus* (see Küng, 1967, ch. 6).

However, this view faces a difficulty. Since particulars are substances, the fundamental particulars are substances. It must therefore be at least logically possible that they should exist independently of other fundamental particulars. Such isolated fundamental particulars, however, would be bare particulars, exemplifying no universals whatsoever. The question arises whether we can admit even the logical possibility of such particulars. If, as we have argued in ch. 11 § 1, it is possible to draw only a "formal distinction" between the logically inseparable aspects of particularity and universality in a particular, then such particulars will be inadmissible. It would also be necessary to reject for such a case the *Principle of Particularization* put forward in ch. 18 § 1. According to this principle, for each particular there must exist one monadic universal which makes the particular just *one* thing. Lacking such a universal, we do not have just one particular.

I believe, therefore, that we ought to reject this way of trying to develop a Relational Realism. But there seems to be no incoherence in the view that the properties of particulars all dissolve *ad infinitum* into structural properties. It has already been argued (ch. 15 § 1) that it is logically possible that there are no simple properties. The same may be asserted of all universals. It is an obvious and plausible extension of this rejection of the view that there *must* be simple universals, to suggest that every monadic universal is analysable as a relationally structural property. Properties will then dissolve *ad infinitum*. All relations will have *terms*, particulars which they relate, but the only properties that these particulars have will themselves be constituted by relations between the further parts of these particulars. The only *natures* in such a world would seem to be relations, and so Relational Realism would be true. This picture of the world seems to be a logical and epistemic possibility. I record that it was noted as a possibility by Donald Williams (1966, pp. 259–61).

There is one difficulty for Relational Realism which seems not to be very serious, but which it may be advisable to get out of the way. We have noted that there are properties which are structural but which are not relationally structural. Thus, suppose that *being an F* is a property. *Being three Fs* would also be a property, a structural property, but not a relationally structural property, of certain particulars (the particular that is the aggregate of three Fs). Is not such a property an exception to the hypothesis that every property is a relationally structural property?

The point must be acknowledged, but the counter-instances seem to be trivial ones. For, in general, where a particular has the structural property, *being three Fs*, then the three parts of the particular will stand in certain relations. And so the very same particular will have a property, *being three Fs related in certain ways*. This *is* a relationally structural property. The property will have as a part the property, *being three Fs*. Furthermore, the property, *being an F*, may be in its turn a relationally structural property. If all these conditions obtain, it is not very impressive to point to the fact that *being three Fs* is not a relationally structural property.

It is logically possible for a subject of predication to have the property, *being three Fs*, and for these three things not to be linked by genuine relations (relations which are universals) in any way.

But for this to happen, at least one necessary condition is that these things be in different space-times. The "aggregate" of three such things, I have already suggested (in ch. 18 § 1), is not a particular.

So, with trivial qualifications, it seems possible that all properties should turn out to be relationally structural properties.

Before leaving this topic we may take brief notice of what may be Leibniz's view that there are no genuine relations, but only properties: monadic universals but no unanalysable polyadic universals. It may be called Monadic Realism. We shall see shortly that, just as some monadic universals can be analysed in terms of polyadic universals, so some polyadic universals can be analysed in terms of monadic universals. I would grant, furthermore, that it is logically possible that every polyadic universal should be analysable in terms of monadic universals. But I deny that it is an epistemic possibility. Whether or not there are simple things in the world, there certainly are complex things. And again, whether or not there are properties irreducible to relations, there certainly are relations which are irreducible to non-relational properties of the related things.

## iv *Internal and External Relations*

In the *Treatise*, Bk. 1 Part 1 § v Hume suggests that every relation there is may be brought under one of seven different heads: *resemblance, identity, relations of time and place, proportion in quantity or number, degree in any quality, contrariety* and *causation*.

He then makes a famous classification of the seven types of relation:

> into such as depend entirely upon the ideas, which we compare together, and such as may be changed without any change in the ideas.

The first sort he calls "relations of ideas". He places in this group *resemblance, proportion in quantity and number, degree in any quality* and *contrariety*. The other three he calls "matters of fact".

I take it that the later distinction, familiarized by the Absolute Idealists, between *internal* and *external* relations, is essentially the same distinction. Since Hume's terminology is unsatisfactory, I will use the latter pair of terms. Donald Williams (1963), after redrawing the distinction, speaks of "intrinsic" and "extrinsic" relations.

I propose the following definitions:

(1) Two or more particulars are *internally* related if and only if there exist properties of the particulars which logically necessitate that the relation holds.

(2) Two or more particulars are *externally* related if and only if there are no properties of the particular which logically necessitate that the relation, or any relation which is part of the relation, holds.

It will be seen that these definitions allow for "mixed" cases, partially internal and partially external relations.

Notice that it is perfectly possible for there to be predicates which apply to each of the internally related particulars, for the predicates to apply in virtue of the properties which necessitate the internal relation, and yet for it not to be necessitated by the predicates alone that the relation holds. Suppose, for instance, that the predicates fail to analyse the properties involved to a depth sufficient to bring out the internality of the relation (for "analysing" predicates see ch. 17). It will be a contingent proposition that particulars falling under those predicates have that relation. Yet the relation may still be internal. This is an important reason for rejecting Hume's phrase "relation of ideas". It is true, of course, that in such cases there will always be *possible* analysing predicates which, when supplied, will necessitate the internal relation.

The definition of an internal relation may be thought to be defective. The term "properties" in the definition must include relational properties. This is because, for instance, two particulars may resemble each other in virtue of a common relational property, and resemblance must be accounted an internal relation, if any relation is. But now consider a father and his child. The relation between them is a causal one and so presumably external. But, it seems, the father will have relational properties which make him 'father of *c*' and the child will have relational properties which make him 'child of *f*'. Does not this make the relation an internal one by our definition?

This objection is met by noting that *being a father of c* cannot be a property, even a relational property. For the corresponding predicate is impure. It involves essential reference to a particular: *c*. To get anything like a genuine relational *property* (a universal), we must go to *being a father of a child*. But it does not follow from the

fact that *f* is the father of a child that *f* is father of the particular child
*c*. By contrast, suppose that *f* is father of a child and *g* is father of a
child. It follows that *f* and *g* stand in the internal relation of
*resemblance in a certain respect*.

Having drawn the distinction between internal and external relations, a reductive thesis may now be proposed. It may be called
*The Reductive Principle for internal relations*:

> If two or more particulars are internally related, then the relation
> is nothing more than the possession by the particulars of the
> properties which necessitate the relation.

In § 1 it was argued that although relational properties are real, they
are reducible (to non-relational properties and relations). It is now
being argued that internal relations are reducible to properties of the
related terms. (These properties may include relational properties,
and so relations. But the relational properties will not necessitate any
irreducible relation between the "related" terms.) External relations,
on the other hand, involve irreducible relations holding between the
externally related particulars. (Monads could have internal, but not
external, relations.)

How is the Reductive Principle to be defended? The usual arguments against postulating an excess of universals may be proposed.
First, it is surely suspicious that, given the properties in question,
the corresponding internal relations are necessitated. An *a posteriori*
Realism will naturally consider that it is too easy a way to discover
the existence of certain relations between particulars simply to
know *properties* of these particulars. Second, there seems to be no
reason to attribute causal efficacy to the relations. For instance, a
sorting machine which detects resemblance in a certain respect is
simply "moved" by the properties of the objects in virtue of which
the objects resemble each other. It is, of course, important that the
objects all have the same sort of effect upon the machine. But the
*"relation of similarity"* is detected *via* the effects of individual particulars, acting in virtue of their properties. By contrast, if *a* pre-
cedes *b*, the fact that this relation obtains may make its own causal
contribution over and above the properties of *a* and *b*.

We have already noted that the relations between predicates and
universals may be many and various. We now see that a many-place
predicate need not apply in virtue of polyadic universals. For in the
case of internal relations an *n*-place predicate may apply in virtue of

*monadic* universals attaching to the *n* particulars. (If the properties involved are relational properties, then the situation is more complex.) With external relations, however, a many-place predicate applies in virtue of irreducibly polyadic universals.

So we can have one-place predicates applying in virtue of monadic universals. We can have many-place predicates applying in virtue of polyadic universals. We can have many-place predicates applying in virtue of monadic universals. Considerations of symmetry suggest that there ought to be one-place predicates which apply in virtue of polyadic universals.

The pure predicate 'heap' is, or is close to being, an example. The predicate applies in virtue of spatial relations of juxtaposition which the *parts* of the heap have. The predicate gives us only minimum information about the non-relational properties of these particulars. Another example, suggested by Jim Franklin, is the predicate 'cluster'.

The moral is, yet again, that the surface structure of a predicate is no infallible guide to the structure of the universals in virtue of which the predicate applies.

A second, and stronger, reductive thesis which I wish to defend about internal relations is that they depend solely upon an identity or partial identity holding between the properties of the particulars entering into the relation. It is clear that this is sometimes the case. *a*'s being F and *b*'s being F determine that *a* and *b* have some resemblance. It would be a great theoretical simplification if it could be shown that an identity of this sort always obtains in the case of internal relations. Furthermore, it would give a clear and simple reason why the internal relation must hold and why it is reducible to the related things having certain properties. Unfortunately, however, this thesis faces a number of objections. I think that they can be answered but cannot answer them until the next Part.

Having defined the notion of internal relation, and advanced two theses about the nature of such relations without defending the second thesis, we can now ask if Hume's "relations of ideas" are genuine internal relations. It seems clear that *resemblance, proportion in number* and *degree in any quality* are internal. (*Contrariety* we may perhaps ignore. Hume says that the only ideas which are in themselves contrary are existence and non-existence.) *Proportion in quantity* may not be so clear. For it is sometimes maintained that the relative size of, say, this elephant and this mouse is determined, not by their properties, but by some relation between them not dependent upon their nature. If this dubious doctrine could be maintained, relations of size would simply have to be reclassified as external. The distinction between internal and external relations is controlled by its definition, not by its paradigms.

An interesting and difficult question arises in the case of *identity*. Hume is thinking of *identity through time*, that relation which holds between different temporal phases of the same thing. He simply assumes that such phases are externally related. And if the phases are particulars, as they seem to be, it certainly does not follow from the properties of the two particulars that they are phases of the same thing. However, there are philosophers who hold that numerically different phases of the same thing are, or can be in favourable cases such as atoms and souls, strictly identical. A Nominalist, as Hume is, is not likely to make much sense of the notion of an identity across numerically different phases. But once universals are admitted, and so it is recognized that different particulars can be identical in certain respects, the way is open to argue a different but parallel thesis: that numerically different phases might be strictly identical in respect of the thing which they were phases of. Such an identity would not flow from the properties of the phases and so would not be an internal relation in terms of our definition. But because the "relation" would flow from an identity it would seem reasonable to extend the conception of an internal relation to cover this case.

I do not accept this account of identity through time. While admitting the possibility of such an account, I find no need to postulate this third type of identity. But I did want to indicate how difficult it may be to decide in particular cases whether we are dealing with an internal or an external relation.

### v  *What relations are there?*

Internal relations are reducible to properties, external relations are not. What sorts of irreducible relation are there in the world? To ask this question is to move outside first philosophy, which is the concern of this work. In Donald Williams' terminology (1953, p. 74), it is to pass from analytic ontology to speculative cosmology. Nevertheless, it is a question of great interest, and it will illuminate our central enquiry if we consider it briefly.

The first question which we can ask is whether Hume's seven

headings really cover the field of relations. I think that it is plausible to say that they very nearly do, although I would add to them *law-like connection*. I shall be arguing in ch. 24 that *causality* is a particular species of law-like connection, but that law-like connection itself is something more than constant conjunction. (By contrast, Hume held that all law-like connection was causal connection. See the *Treatise*, Bk. 1 Part III § 11.) But, in any case, there can be no question of an *a priori* proof that Hume's seven headings suffice.

If they are to suffice, then it may well be necessary to accept some physicalist account of the mind. For non-physical mental processes would seem to involve relations of a radically different sort. But the physicalist can be content with Hume's list, or something like it. It is ironic that Hume himself is not a physicalist.

Hume's list may then be purged of the "relations of ideas", the internal relations. Assuming that relative size and relative duration are internal, we are then left with his three sorts of "matters of fact" or external relation: *"identity"*, *relations of time and place, causation.*

Hume holds, and I think it is plausible to hold, that the "identity" of different phases of the same thing is no more identity than the relation between different spatial parts of the same thing. The question then arises whether an account can be given of the unity of the phases in terms of other relations on Hume's list. It seems that we can appeal to *spatio-temporal continuity, resemblance* and *causation*. Distinct temporal phases of the same object are continuous in space and time. The distinct phases retain many of the same properties, or, where there is change, the property-change is regularly of a continuous nature. (To the extent that *resemblance* is involved, to that extent internal relation is involved.) More important, I believe, than the relations between the phases of *spatio-temporal continuity* and *resemblance*, is the fact that the phases stand in close *causal* relations to each other, the existence of the earlier phases being a causally necessary condition for the existence of the later phases. Such relations between the phases may then be taken to be *constitutive* of identity through time. Working along these familiar lines, made familiar by Hume among others, there seems to be good hope of giving a reductive account of Humean "identity".

We are then left with spatio-temporal relations and causation. Hume himself tried to reduce the ontological component of causation to spatio-temporal relations ("constant conjunction") holding between things of the same sort (for us, things having the same properties). If he had admitted law-like connection in addition to causation, he would have tried to reduce it in the same way. If we follow Hume here, then a remarkable simplification is achieved. The only irreducible polyadic universals which we require to postulate are spatio-temporal relations. It is a striking and simple hypothesis in speculative cosmology.

However, I believe that Hume's view of causation must be rejected. Causation, I agree with Hume, is law-like connection. But in ch. 24 it will be argued that law-like connection is a matter of relations which hold between *universals* rather than particulars ("second-order relations"). One universal necessitates another. *Being F* necessitates *being G*. This necessitation is not logical necessitation, but neither is it reducible to constant conjunction between particulars (e.g. events) having certain properties. Given that a plurality of particulars have certain properties, then it may be *necessitated* that one or more of these particulars should have or acquire certain properties and/or relations. This non-logical necessitation entails a constant conjunction at the level of first-order particulars (with reservations still to be made), but the constant conjunction does not entail the necessitation.

What may be the correct position is this: *first-order* relations, relations between first-order particulars, are all reducible to spatio-temporal relations. Clearly, this hypothesis has close connections with the hypothesis of *Naturalism* (see ch. 12), that the world is in fact nothing but a spatio-temporal world.

Notice that this hypothesis would be compatible with the view that spatio-temporal relations are themselves not ultimate but are analysable in terms of non-spatio-temporal relations. It may be that at some deep level of scientific analysis we come to particulars which are not spatio-temporal and spatio-temporally related. These particulars and their relations would yield the spatio-temporal manifold at a relatively "macroscopic" level. Spatio-temporal particulars and their spatio-temporal relations would be real but not fundamental. As far as I can understand, the present state of subatomic physics makes this possibility a live intellectual option.

We may also wonder, speculatively, just how firm is the distinction suggested in this section between the spatio-temporal relations of particulars, and the relations between universals which constitute causal and other nomic connections. There is, after all, a tradition in philosophy and in science which tries to give an account of certain spatio-temporal relations, at least, in terms of causal relations. For instance, order in time has been thought to depend upon causal order.

But having glanced at these issues, we must now return to the task of analytic ontology.

## VI *Particulars are never reflexively related*

In this work relations and polyadic universals have been identified. The only monadic universals which we have recognized are properties. These assumptions entail that no relation ever relates less than two particulars, and so that no particular can be related to itself. But these assumptions require to be argued for. Many philosophers have held that particulars can stand in relations to themselves.

It was noted at the beginning of this chapter that Russell sometimes speaks of "monadic relations". One might expect him to use the phrase to refer to putative relations, such as *identity*, which always relate a particular to itself. (The term "reflexive relation" seems best restricted to such cases. A relation which relates a particular to itself in some cases but not in others is hardly a "reflexive relation".) In fact, however, Russell is referring to properties! I do not think that he would have considered calling a reflexive relation a monadic relation. The reason is that reflexive relations still require to be symbolized by a *two*-place predicate, even although the places are filled by two tokens of the same referring expression. Given Russell's largely unthinking adoption of a one–one correlation between predicates and universals, it is easy for him to think that what is involved in reflexivity is an eccentric case of a dyadic rather than a monadic universal. Hochberg (1969, p. 173) points out that this confusion is connected with the ambiguity of the word "term". There are two "terms" in the predicate, despite the fact that the predicate only applies to one "term".[1]

It is, of course, obvious that there are linguistic expressions

---

[1] The intellectual tensions involved are excellently illustrated by McTaggart (1921, § 80), who writes:

For a relation *always connects something with something* [McT's italics]. Even when it only connects something with itself, the term so connected with itself is – to use a metaphor which is not, I think, misleading – at both ends of the relation, and this does involve a certain aspect of plurality, though not, of course, a plurality of substances. This may be more obvious if we notice that it is impossible to express any relation without either having two terms, or using one term twice.

having the form 'Raa', for instance, 'He killed himself'. The existence of such expressions constitutes a *prima facie* case for saying that particulars may be related to themselves in various ways. However, given our general position on the way that predicates stand to universals, such a case can be no more than *prima facie*.

If we consider cases actually proposed when a thing is said to be related to itself, then a number of the cases exhibit the now familiar disadvantage that we can determine *a priori*, without any need for empirical investigation, that the particular has that "relation" to itself. We know *a priori* that a particular is *identical* with itself, *resembles* itself, is *the same size* as itself, and so on.[1]

A second argument against such relations, now equally familiar, is that they appear to bestow no causal power upon the particulars which are said to have them.

There are, however, cases against which these two objections do not hold. Most of the natural examples apply to persons: somebody can *love, hate, kill, wash* or *contradict* himself as well as other people. However, persons are not always involved. Ropes can be *entangled with* themselves as well as with other objects. Should we admit that in some or all of these cases a thing really is related to itself?

However, in all such cases, it does seem rather easy to give an account of the ontology of the situations involved without invoking any such relations. One part of a rope is entangled with *another part* of the same rope. One hand washes another; both wash the rest of the body. Perhaps the trickiest sort of case is that where a person loves or hates himself. But even here genuine self-relation seems avoidable. If a man loves himself, then it is not that self-loving state which he loves, but other aspects of himself. It is possible that he should love the self-loving state, but this seems to demand a new, second-order, loving state which is distinct from the original one. At no point do we need to assume that the situation is genuinely reflexive, nor does it appear that such an assumption would have any explanatory value. Occam's Razor then suggests that we should not make the assumption.

There is, however, a difficulty in the case of relations which are

---

[1] See Antony's remarks to Lepidus about the crocodile in Shakespeare's *Antony and Cleopatra* (Act II, scene VII):
"It is shaped sir, like itself, and it is as broad as it hath breadth: it is just as high as it is, and moves with its own organs."
The final phrase was a falling away from tautology, but Antony goes on to point out that it is also of its own colour.

both transitive and symmetrical. Given these characteristics, it can apparently be deduced that the relation is reflexive: objects which have the relation to other things have it to themselves. If time is circular, then *before* is not simply transitive, it is symmetrical. It appears to follow that any temporal event is before itself.

However, we are not forced to this conclusion. Given that:

(1) if xRy, then yRx

and

(2) if xRy and yRz, then xRz

where '*x*', '*y*' and '*z*' are suitably bound variables, then it makes for simpler rules of substitution if we allow *unrestricted* substitution within the range of the variables. Given xRy, by (1) we are also given yRx and can assert xRy and yRx. But if *x* can be substituted for *z*, then xRy and yRx instantiate the antecedent of (2). Hence we can conclude that if xRy, then xRx. If *x* has R to anything, then it has it to itself.

This certainly shows that it is convenient to *say* that the predicate 'having R to *x*' applies to *x* for all *x*. But we could instead stipulate in the definition of transitivity and symmetry that *x*, *y* and *z* must each be different particulars in all cases. This would prevent the deduction of reflexivity. Furthermore, because of the arguments already advanced, this would seem to be the least misleading procedure from the point of view of ontology, whatever its inconvenience for the logician. Alternatively, we can allow the deduction but deny that 'having R to *x*' applies to *x* in virtue of a *relation* in the world which *x* has to itself. It would be a predicate which applies, but not in virtue of any universal.

I conclude that, as a matter of ontology, no particular is related to itself.[1] One consequence of so concluding is the rejection of any doctrine of *causa sui*.

## VII *Final remarks on relations*

Two points conclude this chapter.

The previous section has indirectly brought up an important question. Suppose that a universal is *n*-adic with respect to a particular instantiation of that universal. Could it be *m*-adic with respect to some other instantiation, where $m \neq n$?

[1] This conclusion is also reached by Jørgenson (1953). His view is discussed by Katsoff (1955) and Jørgenson replies (1955).

Tentatively, I suggest that we should accept a *Principle of Instantial Invariance*:

> For all n, if a universal is n-adic with respect to a particular instantiation, then it is n-adic with respect to all its instantiations (it is n-adic *simpliciter*).

The argument for the Principle is simple, and seems to me to be compelling, though it may not be conclusive. A universal is strictly identical in its different instances. But how can it be strictly identical if, in its different instances, it instantiates a different number of particulars?[1]

If the Principle is correct, then it furnishes us with a reason for saying that most alleged cases of self-relation are not genuine. A man may be said to love himself, but the universal, or disjunctive range of universals, in virtue of which the predicate 'loves' applies would appear to be *dyadic* universals. The only putative cases of reflexive relation left standing by the Principle of Instantial Invariance would be such things as *identity* which, if it is a relation, can never have anything but a reflexive exemplification. But other arguments against admitting *identity* as a genuine universal are very strong.

Before concluding the chapter, I would like to recall what was said in ch. 15 § III about the logical equivalence of 'aRb' and 'bR̆a'. The conclusion drawn was that, speaking ontologically, there is no such thing as a relation and its converse. There is simply the one relation holding between *a* and *b*, the particular *a* playing one role in the relational situation and *b* another. Even this difference of roles is only involved for the cases where 'R' ≠ 'R̆'.

But suppose that 'R' ≠ 'R̆'. Professor L. Goddard has asked the question what then is the relation? Is it R or R̆? I think that all that can be said is that to the one relation there correspond the two equally good "naming" predicates: 'R' and 'R̆'.

---

[1] Butchvarov (1966, ch. 3) uses what is in effect the Principle of Instantial Invariance to try to show that resemblance (between universals) is not a genuine relation.

# PART SIX

# THE ANALYSIS OF RESEMBLANCE
# 20
# *The resemblance of particulars*

In ch. 5 we saw that a Resemblance analysis cannot solve the Problem of Universals. In ch. 19 § v, it was argued that, although 'resembles' is a many-place predicate, it does not apply in virtue of any irreducible relation. But, of course, none of this abolishes the fact of resemblance. There is such a fact and any full philosophy of universals must give an account of it. To give such an account is the object of this Part.

The literature of this topic (and there is an interesting and important literature) generally maintains, quite correctly I believe, that there are two main sorts of resemblance. First, there is *the resemblance of particulars*. This is not a particularly taxing topic, and will be considered in the present, relatively brief, chapter. But, second, there is *the resemblance of universals*. We considered one such resemblance in ch. 6, when, following Arthur Pap, we noted that the proposition that *redness* resembles *orangeness* more than *redness* resembles *blueness* states a resemblance-relation holding between certain properties or ranges of properties: a fact which Nominalists find it very difficult to give an account of. The resemblance of universals has proved an extremely difficult and vexing question. The difficulties will be explored in ch. 21 and a new solution proposed in ch. 22.

My conclusion in this Part will be a traditional one: that resemblance is always *identity of nature*. This identity is partial in partial resemblance, and complete in complete resemblance. But in discussing the resemblance of universals I will work out this old doctrine in a new way which, I hope, will meet traditional objections.

## 1 *The resemblance of particulars*

A philosophy which admits objective properties and relations will naturally seek to give an account of the resemblance of particulars in terms of properties and relations. For instance, the resemblance of *a* and *b* on the one hand, to *c* and *d* on the other, might be constituted by the fact that *a* has R to *b* while *c* has R to *d*. To simplify matters, however, the discussion will be confined to the resemblance of *two* particulars, because then the analysis proceeds in terms of properties alone.

I suggest (not very originally) that a particular *a* resembles a particular *b* if and only if:

> There exists a property, P, such that a has P, and that there exists a property, Q, such that b has Q, and *either* P $=$ Q *or* P resembles Q.

P's resembling Q will, of course, be a matter of the resemblance of universals, and so we cannot gain a full view of the resemblance of particulars until we understand the resemblance of universals. But if we are willing to take the latter as a primitive notion for the present (and at least it is a notion which we seem to have some intuitive grasp of), then the present discussion can proceed.

It is important to see that, given our account of properties, this analysis of the resemblance of particulars sets definite limits to points or respects of resemblance. This seems to be as it should be. Consider the following case. It is true of, say, a particular book and a particular flint that neither of them is an apple. The predicate 'not an apple' applies to them both. But, unless in the grip of philosophical theory, I think that we should be most reluctant to say that this was a point or respect of *resemblance* between the book and the flint. It is not really something which they have in common. Our reluctance is not simply due to the fact that it is an insignificant truth about the two objects that they are not apples. It is an insignificant truth about the two objects that they are both material solids. But I think that we would allow that this latter was an (insignificant) point or respect of resemblance.

These facts are explained, and in accordance with our analysis of resemblance, if we remember that 'not being an apple' does not apply to different particulars in virtue of identical or even resembling properties. 'Being material', however, may well apply in virtue of the one property or at least in virtue of resembling properties.

Henry Monsour has objected that we would be prepared to say that two persons resemble each other in being blind, but that 'blind' appears to be as much a negative predicate as 'not being an apple'. However, 'blind' does not just have the force 'not having the power of sight'. If it did, stones and explosions would be blind. To be blind, objects must be of the sort which normally have sight. They therefore have that much resemblance. But, more than this, blindness is a momentous thing in human and animal life. Much flows from it in the way of positive conduct, and much of this much exhibits resemblances. So 'blind' is not so clearly a negative predicate. However, perhaps it should be admitted that, where the applicability of a predicate is considered of great importance, we will speak of "resemblance" even where there is no genuine common property or genuine resemblance of universals.

It is easy to extend our analysis to cover other statements of the resemblance of particulars. "*a* and *b* have no resemblance whatsoever" will, if taken literally, simply be the denial of common property or resemblance of universals. Normally, however, the speaker who utters this sentence will have in mind a limited (perhaps ill-defined) range or ranges of properties to which his variables are restricted. Again, "*a* resembles *b* exactly", if taken literally will become 'For all properties, P, *a* has P if and only if *b* has P'. *a* and *b*, though not identical, will be identical in *nature*. But in ordinary discourse the scope of "P" will usually be restricted in some (perhaps ill-defined) way.

It is interesting to notice that this definition of exact resemblance has the consequence that two "bare particulars", if such things could exist, would resemble each other exactly. The formula would hold vacuously, because neither would have any properties. I do not think that this consequence is counter-intuitive.

What of *degrees* of resemblance between particulars? The natural way to analyse such statements as '*a* resembles *b* more than *a* resembles *c*' seems to be either in terms of the *relative number* of properties which *a* and *b*, and *a* and *c*, have in common with each other respectively, or else the relative number of properties which, although not identical, resemble each other relatively closely.

It is obvious how much room for vagueness and/or relativity there is in this formula. For instance, our discussion of conjunctive properties in ch. 15 has shown us that the numbering of properties can be just as arbitrary as the numbering of particulars. So statements about the degree of resemblance of particulars may presuppose a list or other criteria of what is to count as "one property" or "one range of properties" in such situations. This list or other criteria will usually reflect something as ontologically unimportant as our practical concerns. Practical concerns may also lead us to distinguish between important and not-so-important respects of resemblance and to weight the comparisons accordingly.

I believe that this is about as much as needs to be said by way of a positive account of the resemblance of particulars. But two objections to the account require to be considered.

## 11 *An epistemological difficulty*

The analysis given of the resemblance of particulars is a variant of the "Respect" account. (The respect in our analysis is a property or resemblance between properties.) But all such analyses are exposed to a difficulty which has troubled some philosophers (for instance, Aaron, 1939). It is possible to recognize resemblances and yet to be unable to detect in what respect the particulars concerned resemble each other. It may be clear to us that two faces resemble each other in some way (beyond being faces!), but we may be unable to discern what that way is. Such phenomena have been thought to cast doubt upon the view that the resemblance of particulars is always resemblance in a respect.

However, as was already recognized by Thomas Reid (1941 edition, p. 310), such phenomena are at least *compatible* with a Respect analysis. First, it may be that in the recognition of resemblance of faces we do have some awareness of a respect of resemblance, although an awareness which is vague and which perhaps could not be put into words. Second, even if such awareness is consciously lacking, it might still be the case that we were unconsciously aware of the respect. But third, and most important, even if both inarticulate and unconscious awareness of a respect is lacking, it might yet be the case that the resemblance which we were aware of was *in fact* resemblance in a certain respect.

Suppose that we are aware of a resemblance between two things but that we are not aware of, whether consciously, half-consciously or unconsciously, any respect of resemblance. The two things are likely to have many different respects of resemblance. The difficulty then is to say which of these respects constitutes the resemblance of which we are aware.

Suppose that one of these respects is the respect R. Suppose that it is the particular's possession of R which is responsible (in general, causally responsible) for our awareness that the two things resemble each other in an unknown respect. Then, and only then, I suggest, can we say that that unknown respect is in fact R.

Such recognition of resemblance unaccompanied by any recognition of the respect of the resemblance poses no problem for a scientific psychology. J. J. C. Smart has pointed out that it is in fact easier to design machines which will "recognize" that objects resemble each other in some respect than machines which will "identify" that respect (1963, pp. 655–6). A pair of scales provides a helpful analogy. Scales can "recognize" that two things are of the same or different weights, but cannot by the mere device of balancing weights "identify" the absolute weights of the particulars involved. It is easy to understand that a human perceiver may be sensitive to the likeness or unlikeness of respects within some range, yet be insensitive to the point on the range occupied by the things perceived or even to the general nature of the range.

None of this *shows* that when we recognize a resemblance among particulars, but cannot recognize the respect of the resemblance, that there is in fact a respect involved. But suppose that we have independent grounds for holding resemblance between particulars always to be resemblance in some respect. We can then rather easily explain how it is possible nevertheless to detect resemblance, yet utterly fail to detect the respect of the resemblance.

### III *Sense-data and resemblance*

A problem is sometimes raised about the resemblance of those controversial particulars: sense-data. Suppose sense-datum *a* to be indistinguishable in colour from sense-datum *b*, and *b* to be indistinguishable in colour from sense-datum *c*. In the circumstances, it has been claimed, it is possible for *a* and *c* to be distinguishable. Suppose, for instance, that the sense-data are obtained by looking at three pieces of cloth which are each dyed a very slightly different shade of some colour. Sense-data *a* and *b* may appear to be indistinguishable in colour and so, it is often argued, actually indistinguishable. The same may hold for sense-data $b$ and $c$. But $a$ and $c$ may be distinguishable. So $a$ and $b$ exactly resemble each other in colour, and so do $b$ and $c$; yet $a$ and $c$ do not.

Now, if this situation can really obtain, it is impossible to analyse the exact resemblance of the three sense-data in terms of their having an identical property. For, like all identity, property-identity is transitive, yet in this situation the exact resemblance is not transitive.

But we need not give up the transitivity of exact resemblance. There are in fact at least two other possible ways of analysing the situation. First, we can distinguish between $a$ and $b$ (and $b$ and $c$) resembling exactly and our being unable to detect any failure of resemblance. We could then say that the sense-data were of different shades of colour, and so had different properties, but that we were unable to detect the difference. This involves allowing that sense-data can have undetectable characteristics. Second, we can take the whole case to be an argument for saying that there are no such particulars as sense-data and so no question about the nature of their resemblance. I believe that this second response is in fact the correct one.

# 21

# *The resemblance of universals (I): criticism of received accounts*

Having given an account of the resemblance of particulars we must now consider the far more difficult and complex question of the resemblance of universals. We may begin by noting various cases where we are inclined to assert such a resemblance. The cases are all cases of properties. This restriction of our examples to monadic universals makes for simplicity. I do not think that it will affect the generality of the conclusions reached.

The different shapes resemble each other: they are all shapes. Furthermore, one (sort of) shape may resemble another more closely than it resembles a third. *Triangularity* is more like *quadrilaterality* than it is like *circularity*. The different colours resemble each other: they are all colours. Furthermore, one colour may resemble another more closely than it resembles a third. *Redness* is more like *orangeness* than it is like *blueness*. Different tastes may resemble each other in being cloying, different smells in being acrid, or different colours in being "warm". Granted that the (different sorts of) games are not accounted games in virtue of something identical, nevertheless they do have a resemblance.

Our task is to give an account of resemblances such as these. Different accounts have been proposed by philosophers. (1) There is the attempt to *reduce* such resemblances to propositions about particulars. (2) There is the attempt to account for the resemblances in terms of *second-order properties*: common properties of the universals concerned. (3) There is the attempt to account for the resemblances in terms of *second-order relations*: relations holding between the universals concerned. (4) There is the attempt to account for the resemblances by drawing the distinction between *determinables* and *determinates*. (5) There is the sceptical attempt to account for the resemblances as subjective phenomena. These accounts do not necessarily conflict, because different cases of the resemblance of universals may be analysed in different ways.

In this chapter reasons will be given for rejecting each of these accounts, at least as accounts of the whole range of the resemblances to be accounted for. The chapter ends on this negative note. But it clears the ground for a new account of the resemblance of universals, an account which is given in the next chapter.

## 1 *Reduction of the resemblance of universals to propositions about particulars*

It would be a major theoretical simplification if an account could be given of the apparent resemblance of universals in terms of the properties and relations of mere (first-order) particulars. Such an account appears possible in some cases.

Suppose that two (sorts of) taste resemble each other in that they are both cloying. We have:

(1)   $T_1$ cloys and $T_2$ cloys

A plausible attempt to analyse the situation is:

(1')   For all particulars, x, if x has $T_1$ or x has $T_2$, then x cloys.

It is, of course, unlikely that there is a genuine property, *cloyingness*. But the predicate 'cloys' will apply to particulars in virtue of various properties, including perhaps relational properties, of the particulars.

There is, however, a justified complaint against this analysis. It fails to do justice to the link between the tastes of the substances and the fact that the substance cloys. Something of the following sort is therefore required:

(1'') For all particulars, x, if x has $T_1$ or x has $T_2$, then *as a causal result of x being $T_1$ or $T_2$*, x cloys.

This addition does entail the consequence that to say that a taste is cloying involves a causal hypothesis. But this consequence does not seem objectionable.

If this is satisfactory, then we can also analyse:

(2)   $S_1$ is acrid and $S_2$ is acrid

as

(2')   For all particulars, x, if x has $S_1$ or x has $S_2$, then as a causal result of x being $S_1$ or $S_2$, x produces a characteristic sensory irritation in those who smell x.

It may also be possible to analyse:

    (3)  Redness and orangeness are both "warm"

as

    (3')  For all particulars, x, if x is red or x is orange, then, as a causal result of x being red or orange, x produces an association of warmth in the minds of those who see x.

However, this third analysis is controversial. It has been argued that what makes some colours "warm" and other colours "cold" is some deeper resemblance between "warm" colours and *warmth*, on the one hand, and "cold" colours and *coldness*, on the other. The association of ideas would then be a mere effect of this resemblance (see Johnson, 1921, pp. 190–1 and Hayek, 1952, ch. 1 § v). If this is correct, then it is not clear how the resemblance of the "warm" colours is to be reduced to a resemblance among particulars.

However, even if (3') is on the right track, these analyses do not quite achieve their intended effect. In each case, the reference to a causal connection is essential. But it will be argued in ch. 24 that causal connection is a species of nomic connection, and that nomic connection is a matter of *relations between universals*. If that is so, then we have not completely succeeded in analysing the resemblances between universals in terms of properties and relations of particulars.

We may now turn to another group of propositions:

    (4)  Triangularity and circularity resemble each other in being shapes
    (5)  Redness and blueness resemble each other in being colours
    (6)  Triangularity resembles quadrilaterality more than it resembles circularity
    (7)  Redness resembles orangeness more than it resembles blueness.

We have already examined an attempt to reduce such propositions in ch. 6 § 1. In that chapter the attempt at reduction was being made in the interests of Nominalism. The Nominalist wished to get rid of apparent referring expressions such as 'Triangularity' and 'Redness' in favour of mere predicates such as 'triangular' and 'red', preparatory to denying objective properties altogether. But the arguments we advanced against the Nominalist there hold equally now against a Realist who is trying to reduce the "resemblances of universals" to propositions about the properties of particulars.

Let me remind the reader that it is not possible to reduce (5) to:

(5′) For all particulars, x, if x is red or is blue, then x is coloured.

For, as Frank Jackson (1977) has pointed out, comparison of (5) with

(5.1 ) For all particulars, x, if x is red or x is blue, then x is *extended*

shows that (5′) is an undertranslation of (5). For although (5.1) is true,

(5.1′) Redness and blueness are extensions

which is the parallel proposition to (5), is *false*.

Again, as Arthur Pap argued (1959), the attempt to translate (7) as:

(7′) For all particulars, x, y, z, if x is red and y is orange and z is blue, then x resembles y more than x resembles z

fails because (7′) is not even true for all values of $x, y$ and $z$.

An alternative is:

(7″) For all particulars, x, y, z, if x is red and y is orange and z is blue, then x resembles y in colour more than x resembles z in colour.

It was pointed out in ch. 6, however, that 'resembles in colour' cannot be treated as a semantically unanalysable predicate. But if it is treated as semantically complex, then it must apply in virtue of the *resemblance* of the colours in question, which brings the analysis round in a circle.

In no case considered, then, do we appear to be able completely to reduce resemblances of universals to propositions about the properties (and/or relations) of particulars. As a matter of fact, however, this is not the end of the matter. At the end of a long argument, we shall arrive at the surprising conclusion that it is, after all, possible to give an account of (4) to (7) purely in terms of the properties of particulars. That, however, is a matter for the next chapter.

11 *The resemblance of universals as common properties of universals*

Perhaps what is required is to introduce *second-order universals* and, in particular, *second-order properties*? Perhaps not only particulars can have properties, but universals themselves can have properties? Some resemblances of universals, at least, might then be a matter of the universals involved each having the same property.

The most likely candidates are our propositions (4) and (5):

(4)  Triangularity and circularity resemble each other in being shapes

might be translated as:

(4′)  Shaped (*triangularity*) and Shaped (*circularity*)

where (4′) is the second-order equivalent of:

$$Fa \ \& \ Fb.$$

Similarly:

(5)  Redness and blueness resemble each other in being colours

becomes:

(5″)  Coloured (*redness*) and Coloured (*blueness*).

We have still to discuss the question whether universals can fall under universals, that is, whether properties and relations can themselves have properties and relations. This difficult topic will be the subject of the final Part of this book. It is clear that the same *predicate* can apply to an indefinite number of universals. For instance, the predicate 'different from green' applies to *redness* and to *blueness*. Even if *redness* and *blueness* are not properties, yet they seem at least to be ordered classes of properties, and this predicate will apply to each member of the class. But we know at this stage of our argument that the applicability of predicates to universals is very far from showing that universals can fall under universals.

Nevertheless, as will emerge, there are reasons to think that universals do have properties, and so that at least some cases of the "resemblance of universals" are cases where the universals in question have a common property. Suppose that two properties are both complex. They resemble each other in this respect. Although a formal or topic-neutral feature, *complexity* appears to be a feature which is genuinely common to the two properties. It is an *identical* feature of the two properties. (The argument for all this will be developed in ch. 23 § 1.)

Nevertheless, whatever is said about *complexity*, it seems that (4) and (5) cannot be analysed in terms of properties of properties.

One philosopher who apparently held a contrary opinion, at least with respect to (5), was Russell. He wrote (1959):

> I should regard 'red is a colour' as a genuine subject-predicate proposition, assigning to the 'substance' *red* the quality *colour*. (p. 171)

This is not completely clear, because "the 'substance' *red*" may refer not to the universal but to the spatially and temporally scattered particular which is the aggregate of all red things. But I think that Russell is to be interpreted as holding that the property *redness* has the property *being coloured*. Its logical form is C(R).

Two objections may be made to this view. In the first place, it is not the way that we talk. We do not say that *redness* is coloured. Particulars may be coloured, but *redness*, we say, is *a colour*. Ordinary language does not attribute a property to *redness*, but only membership of a class. And as we have constantly emphasized in this work, membership of a class does not automatically bestow a property upon the member. In the same way, *triangularity* is not said to be shaped. Particulars are shaped. *Triangularity is* a shape. It is a member of the class of shapes.

In the second place, not only does *redness* resemble the other colours in being a colour, it also differs from them in colour. *Redness* and *blueness* differ as colours. The property in which they are supposed to resemble each other is the very thing in which they differ. This seems impossible. Things cannot differ in the respect in which they are identical. The conclusion must be that the resemblance of the colours is not a matter of their having a common property.

Similarly, not only does *triangularity* resemble the other sorts of shape, it also differs from them in shape. *Triangularity* and *circularity* differ as shapes. So their resemblance cannot be constituted by a common property.[1]

---

[1] What I have just said is contradicted by G. F. Stout (1930, p. 398):
> The point is that red and yellow do not resemble each other in one character and differ in another. The respect in which they are alike, i.e. colour, is also the respect in which they are dissimilar. The same holds for squareness and roundness.

I think that Stout is trying to maintain a self-contradictory position.

This situation with respect to colours, shapes, etc., was noted by the Absolute Idealists (see, in particular, F. H. Bradley, 1893a, b). They tried to do justice to it by introducing the notion of identity-in-difference. They maintained that the different colours were all (partially) identical, and yet that this identity was also the ground of the difference of the colours. At the same time, unlike Stout in the passage just footnoted, they accepted the point that the notion of identity-in-difference was *ultimately contradictory*. This then gave them a reason for holding that, ultimately, there are no distinct colours or, indeed, after further similar reasonings, anything which is distinct from anything else.

A pluralist philosophy can agree with the Absolute Idealists that identity-in-difference is an incoherent notion. It cannot accept the view that only the One exists. We must therefore draw the conclusion that the resemblance of the colours is not a matter of their having a common, that is, an identical, property.

What prospect is there for analysing:

(6) Triangularity resembles quadrilaterality more than it resembles circularity

(7) Redness resembles orangeness more than it resembles blueness

in terms of properties of properties?

In the first place, it is clear that, just as in the case of (4) and (5), these resemblances cannot be explained by saying that the properties in question have a common property. This was pointed out clearly by the psychologist Stumpf (quoted by William James, 1950 edition, pp. 532–3). Consider the colours. An identical factor in each can do nothing to establish the resemblance-*order* in which they stand. For that in which things are identical, in that they cannot differ. The resemblance-order must be established by *differentiating* factors in each colour.

It seems, then, that if we are going to appeal to properties of properties in analysing (6) and (7), it is to different *numbers* of common properties that we must appeal. We must say that *triangularity* has more properties in common with *quadrilaterality* than it has with *circularity*, or that *redness* has more properties in common with *orangeness* than it does with *blueness*.

In the case of the colours, in particular, we seem to have no notion what these properties might be. However, that difficulty is epistemological only, and, by itself, might not be too serious. Instead, it is the *continuity* of the resemblance-order which sets the real problem. *Redness* is more like one shade of orange than it is like another shade of orange, and one shade of red is more like a certain shade of orange than another shade of red is like that shade of orange, and so on. To do justice to all these degrees of resemblance we will need to provide all these shades with huge numbers of properties. Similar provisions will be required for the shapes. If the colour and shape continua are mathematical continua, then infinities of properties are demanded. It seems an utterly implausible account of the nature of these resemblance-orders.

Hence, although there may be some cases where the resemblance of universals *is* a matter of their possessing common properties, in the cases of shapes and colours the resemblance of universals cannot be analysed in terms of common properties.

### III *The resemblance of universals as the relations of universals*

If the appeal to second-order properties fails, then perhaps an appeal to second-order *relations* may succeed. For example, perhaps:

(7)    Redness resembles orangeness more than it resembles blueness

has the form:

(7‴)    R (*redness, orangeness, blueness*)

where R is some three-term relation holding between these three terms.

Such a view has been defended by R. W. Church (1952), though for a less fully-worked-out version, see Blanshard (1939 chs. 16 and 17, and 1962, ch. 9). According to Church propositions like (7) testify to the existence of a certain fundamental *order* among certain classes of properties. In the order of the colours, *redness* and *orangeness* lie relatively close together, *redness* and *blueness* relatively far apart. Again, to say of any two colours that they are both colours is simply to say that they both belong to this one order. The order is the fundamental fact. The order creates the class of colours. And an order, of course, is constituted by ordering *relations*.

These ordering relations will, to a great extent, herd universals into a number of mutually exclusive classes. The colours will form one such class, the shapes another, the lengths yet another. The formal nature of the ordering will differ from class to class. For instance, the class of lengths form a one-dimensional continuum. The colours can be ordered, apparently, in a circle, although different possible saturations and intensities of the one hue are matters of one-dimensional ordering. For other classes of universals the formal nature of their order may still have to be determined by phenomenological or other investigation. However, it is not necessary that the ordering-relations create nothing but mutually exclusive classes. There may be orderings which cut across other orderings. Possible examples are the classing of *redness* with *warmth* and *blueness* with *coldness*.

This account of the resemblances of certain classes of universals is an impressive one. It provides a very plausible explanation of degrees of resemblance between certain universals, and also of the principle of unity of such classes as the class of the colours. Furthermore, I think that there are indeed irreducible second-order relations: relations which relate not first-order particulars but universals. Nevertheless, an account such as Church's involves at least three serious difficulties.

(1) In ch. 19 § IV, the notion of an internal relation of particulars was defined. We can also define the notion of an internal relation for universals. Universals are internally related if and only if the relation which holds between them is logically necessitated by the existence of the universals. In the case of particulars it was argued further that the internal "relations" are not something over and above the possession by the particulars of certain properties. In a similar way, internal relations between universals seem to be nothing over and above the universals themselves and their properties.

But now consider the alleged relation between *redness, orangeness* and *blueness*. It appears to be the universals themselves which logically determine the relations of resemblance which hold between them. Put the universals, and their resemblances are automatically determined. The natural conclusion to draw is that, in the sphere of universals as well as the sphere of particulars, 'resembles' is a many-place predicate to which no irreducibly polyadic universal corresponds.

(2) A second difficulty is this. The resemblances of universals of the sort which we have been discussing in this section admit of

degree. This degree has an upper limit in *exact resemblance*. Now, given the general position taken up in this book, at least, exact resemblance can be nothing but *identity*. And identity, we have continually urged, is not a relation.

This gives rise to a problem. How can the relation of resemblance, admitting of degrees, have as its upper limit the non-relation of identity? In the previous chapter we solved this problem with respect to particulars. But we did it by appealing to common properties. It was a matter of the particulars having more and more properties in common, with the limiting case that where they have all properties in common, that is, where they are identical in nature though not identical particulars. But we are at present seeking to analyse the resemblance of universals not in terms of common properties but rather in terms of relations.

(3) A third difficulty is proposed by Kearns (1968, p. 108), criticizing Blanshard.

The suggestion which we are considering is that such classes of universals as the class of shapes or the class of colours are united by the (second-order) relation of resemblance. This relation is, of course, a universal, a one which unites indefinitely many such classes. It is essential, however, that this relation should admit of degree, for shapes, colours, etc. resemble each other more and less closely. As a result, appeal is not really being made to a single second-order relation but rather to a whole class of relations: *the different degrees of resemblance*. The upshot is that we are trying to give an account of the unity of certain classes of first-order universals by means of a class of second-order universals. A principle of unity is still required for the latter. If that principle of unity is a relation of resemblance, as in consistency it should be, then this relation will also have degrees. A vicious infinite regress follows.

It will be seen that Kearns' argument is very similar to Russell's criticism of Resemblance Nominalism (ch. 5 § vi). Russell argues that it is impossible to give an account of the properties of particulars in terms of the relation of resemblance, because the notion of resemblance will again have to be invoked to give an account of what is common to all the resemblances. Kearns' argument, in effect, is that it is impossible to give an account of the unity of certain classes of universals in terms of the (second-order) relation of resemblance because the latter involves the very notion of a resemblance-class of universals which is the notion to be analysed.

It was argued in ch. 5 § VI that even if Russell's regress is not vicious (as I believe that it is vicious), then it is at least uneconomical. The necessity to postulate *a priori* an infinite series of relations of resemblance is a good Occamist argument against Resemblance Nominalism. In the same way, even if Kearns' regress is not logically vicious (as I believe that it is vicious), it is viciously uneconomical. The class consisting of all the different degrees of second-order resemblance would itself have to be unified by third-order resemblances between the members of this class. These resemblances again form a mere class, because they can differ in degree, and this class has to be unified by higher-order resemblances *ad infinitum*. An *a priori* argument for an infinite series of universals must arouse suspicion.

We have now examined three difficulties for the view that the resemblance of such universals as the colours and the shapes is a matter of relations between the universals. Briefly, the objections were these. (a) The so-called relations are internally related to their terms, which suggests that the relations are nothing. (b) The so-called relations admit of degree, with identity as the upper limit of the degree. But it is unclear how the limit of a series of relations could be the non-relation of identity. (c) Finally, the necessity to admit degrees of resemblance between universals means that an account is given of the unity of classes of universals in terms of a class of universals, a class where the same problem of unification is reproduced.

In the next chapter it will be argued that the principle of the unity of such classes as the colours and the shapes does indeed involve certain relations between universals. But the relations are analysable in *first-order* terms.

### IV *Determinables and determinates*

As the reader may be aware, much modern discussion of the particular cases which we have been considering has been dominated by W. E. Johnson's now classical distinction between *determinables* and *determinates* (1921, ch. 11). Let us see what light this distinction can cast upon our problem.

For Johnson, *shape* is a determinable relative to the determinate *triangularity*, and *colour* a determinable relative to the determinate *redness*. He drew attention to three features of the way in which determinables stand to determinates. (a) If a particular has a determinate property, then it is entailed that the particular has the determinable property. Necessarily, if a thing is triangular, it has a shape. Necessarily, if a thing is red, it has a colour. (b) If a particular falls under a determinable, then it is entailed that it has one of the corresponding determinate properties, although it is not entailed which. Necessarily, if a thing has a shape, it has a particular shape. Necessarily, if a thing is coloured, it has a particular colour. (c) The one particular cannot at the same time be qualified by more than one of the determinates which fall under a common determinable. A thing cannot at once be triangular and circular, or red and blue all over.

(This third condition, as it is laid down by Johnson, is not quite accurate. Determinates under a common determinable do not exclude each other in this way unless they are "at the same level". This qualification is necessary because between a determinable and one of its determinates there can be an intermediate. The intermediate is a determinate to the original determinable, but a determinable to the original determinate. *Redness* is a determinate to *colour*, but a determinable to *scarlet*. *Scarlet* is also a determinate of *colour*. But *redness* and *scarlet* do not exclude each other. Exclusion is only guaranteed by determinates of a common determinable which do not stand to each other as determinable to determinate or *vice-versa*. They are then at the same level. See Searle, 1959.)

Not all that Johnson says about determinables and determinates is easy to interpret. But as he is read by Arthur Prior (1949), Johnson takes the exclusiveness of co-determinates at the same level as the essence of the unity of a class of determinates. The unity of the class of shapes or the class of colours is constituted and exhausted by the fact that co-determinates at the same level cannot simultaneously qualify the same particular. These classes are simply classes-of-incompatibles. Suppose that each member of a certain group of people dislikes every other member of the group. The group would be a group-of-incompatibles, a mutual detestation society. This might be the only "unifying" feature of the group. Johnson seems to hold that the class of shapes, the class of colours, etc. are unified in no other way. Their "unifying" incompatibility takes the form of not being prepared to qualify the same particular at the same place and time.

When considering the problem of the resemblance of universals it is most useful to have available the distinction between determinable and determinate, and to be reminded of the incompatibility of such things as the colours. But, as it will now be argued, the distinction at best states, and in no way solves, the problem. In particular, Johnson's account of the way in which classes of determinates are unified is quite inadequate.

First, it is not clear that all sets of universals which exhibit an intrinsic resemblance-order form a set-of-incompatibles. Tastes appear to have an intrinsic resemblance-order. But is it impossible for the very same thing to be simultaneously sweet and sour? Sounds appear to be so ordered. But are they incompatible with each other in the way that shapes and colours are? I do not think that we know the answer to these questions. In ch. 17 it was suggested that we may not know the answer until, and if, tastes and sounds are scientifically identified with, or at least well-correlated with, physical parameters.

Second, Johnson's solution seems to cast no light upon the internal ordering of the shapes, the colours, etc. The incompatibility of *redness, orangeness* and *blueness* does nothing to explain why *redness* is more like *orangeness* than *redness* is like *blueness*. It is true that one might analyse such degrees of resemblance in terms of the "position" of the various shades in the hierarchy of determinables and determinates. (*Colour* being the highest determinable and absolutely specific shades the lowest determinates.) But what determines these "positions"?

Third, Johnson leaves us wondering: "Why do these classes of properties form classes of incompatibles? What is there about the shapes, the colours, etc. which makes them incompatible in this way?" This is the question which we would like to see answered. Johnson's "solution", however, if that is what it is meant to be, is simply a statement of the problem.

Fourth, Johnson's view that co-determinates at the same level have nothing in common except their incompatibility is phenomenologically implausible. The class of shapes or the class of triangles, the class of colours or the class of reds, appear to have much more in common than that.

The solution of the problem of the resemblance of universals is therefore still to be found.

v *Scepticism about the resemblance of universals*

In philosophy or elsewhere, if it proves difficult to give an account of some phenomenon, somebody is sure to suggest that the phenomenon does not exist, or is at least just a "subjective" one. This proves to be the case for the problem of the resemblance of universals.

According to C. W. Hendel (1963, pp. 124–5) Hume took this view of the resemblance of qualitatively different "simple ideas". Referring to the well-known footnote to the *Treatise*, Bk. 1, Part 1, § 7, where Hume discusses the resemblance of *blue*, *green* and and *scarlet*, Hendel says that Hume held that:

> What underlies the finding of such resemblance is the assimilative tendency of the mind itself, and nothing in the perceived things. (p. 125)

I am not convinced by Hendel's reading and incline rather to the view of Church, who holds that Hume is putting forward the view, discussed in § III, that the resemblance is a relation between the qualities, flowing from the nature of the qualities themselves (for Church on Hume, see his 1935, pp. 34–7). But Hendel's interpretation of Hume is also not without plausibility.

Whatever Hume's view was, F. A. Hayek (1952) certainly "solves" the problem of the resemblance of qualities by declaring that resemblance to be an arbitrary classification of the mind. It is true that Hayek has already been quoted in § 1 as resisting the idea that the "resemblance" between, say, *redness* and *warmth* is a mere association of ideas. But Hayek's point is that this resemblance is at exactly the same level as the supposedly more objective order of, say, the colours. Neither, he thinks, is anything more than a physiological *a priori*.

That the ordering of qualities is relative and, apparently, subjective, is also argued for briefly by Nelson Goodman (1970, pp. 28–9). The subjective nature of the ordering is upheld explicitly by Van Steenburgh (1974), although he does note the link between closeness of such resemblance and identity.

It seems to me that this "solution" of the problem is clearly a desperate one, to be embraced only as a last resort. In any case, it seems plausible only with respect to the so-called "secondary qualities". The ordered resemblance of the shapes, for instance, appears to be perfectly objective. This should encourage us to look for an objective solution in the case of the colours also.

·     ·     ·     ·     ·

The results of this chapter have been negative. But, as the reader is now in a position to appreciate, the problem is a very difficult and complex one. Various lines of solution have been proposed by philosophers. None of these solutions succeeds, I have argued, but each involves insights which can, I believe, be built upon.

# 22

# *The resemblance of Universals (II): a new account*

In the last chapter it was argued that some "resemblances of universals" (for instance, the cloyingness of two tastes) are analysable, partially at least, in terms of the common properties of particulars. Some are analysable in terms of common properties of the resembling universals (for instance, that each of the universals is complex). It may well be that universals can be related as well as have properties, and, if so, it is possible that some resemblances among universals flow from these relations. But there are resemblances between universals, in particular between those which may be classified as determinates falling under a common determinable, that appear to defy any of these three forms of treatment. At the same time, these recalcitrant resemblances seem to be objective phenomena, demanding an ontological analysis. The object of this chapter is to provide such an analysis.

What is it that we wish to explain? If we consider the class of the shapes and the class of the colours, then both classes exhibit the following interesting but puzzling characteristics which it would be agreeable to understand:

(a) the members of the two classes all have something in common (they are all shapes, they are all colours)

(b) but while they have something in common, they differ in that very respect (they all differ as shapes, they all differ as colours)

(c) they exhibit a resemblance-order based upon their intrinsic natures (*triangularity* is more like *quadrilaterality* than *triangularity* is like *circularity*, *redness* is more like *orangeness* than *redness* is like *blueness*), where closeness of resemblance has a limit in identity

(d) they form a set-of-incompatibles (the same particular cannot be simultaneously triangular and circular, or red and blue all over).

### 1 *Determinables are not universals*

I begin by denying that there are any *determinable* universals. All genuine universals are *determinates*. There are such predicates as 'coloured' or 'red', but there is no property, *being coloured* or *being red*. To assert that a particular is red is to assert that the particular has some property, a property which is a member of a certain class of properties: the class of all the absolutely determinate shades of red. *a* is red if and only if:

> There is a monadic universal, P, such that a is P and P is a member of the class of the determinate shades of red.

Since human powers of discrimination are relatively limited, this analysis has the consequence that, even when we know that something is red because we can see it, we will seldom, perhaps never, know what actual property the thing has, that is, what determinate shade of red it has. If there are continuum-many determinates falling under a determinable, and all are instantiated, then there will be continuum-many properties associated with this determinable. The class of shades of red is, in turn, a (somewhat vaguely delimited) sub-class of the class of all determinate shades of colour.

Why must it be denied that predicates such as 'red' are property-predicates? In effect, the argument has already been presented in ch. 21 § 11, although there the concern was to show that *colour* is not a property of *redness, blueness*, etc. We now turn to the same line of reasoning directed against the putative property of *redness*.

Suppose that *redness* is a property which all red particulars, whatever their shade of red, have in common. Since properties are universals, this entails that the particulars are *identical* in a certain respect: in respect of their *redness*. Now consider particulars of different shades of red. It is in this very respect of *redness* that they differ. Yet it is impossible that things be identical and different in the very same respect. It is undeniable that different shades of red are different properties. It follows that *redness* is not a property common to all red things.

It must be accepted that nothing can agree and differ in the identical respect. But the great importance of the issue demands that the rest of the argument be considered further. Suppose it be argued that all red things are identical in their *redness*, but that their difference in shade is not difference in *redness*. Now consider the crimson things. They, too, will have a common property. However, if a thing is crimson, then it is entailed that it is red. *Crimsonness* involves *redness*. What is peculiar to crimson things, therefore, must be something less than *crimsonness*. It might be called 'crimsonness-minus-redness', which we can abbreviate as 'C'. (Any other determinable property between *crimsonness* and *redness* must be subtracted also.) It matters not (it may be said) that in a crimson thing the *redness* and the *C-ness* are inseparable. The non-identity of the properties does not entail that they are separable constituents of the property, *being crimson*.

This account would explain very simply both the truth and the necessity of:

(1)   For all particulars, x, if x is crimson, then x is red.

For it would be translated as:

(1′)   For all particulars, x, if x is red and x is C, then x is red.

The difficulty arises instead with:

(2)   Crimson is a shade of red.

We know already (from ch. 6 § 1) that this says more than:

(2′)   For all particulars, x, if x is crimson, then x is red.

Presumably, therefore, (2) must be translated along these lines:

(2″) *Redness and C-ness* is a shade of red.

However, (2″) fails to capture the special relationship required to hold between *redness* and *C-ness*. To see this, consider that there might be a visually observed property, D, co-extensive with C, and yet *redness and D-ness* would not constitute a shade of *redness*.

The point is that the determinable *redness* seems to spread itself out into its determinates, so that mere talk of *redness and C-ness* leaves the connection between the two putative properties far too external to each other. The Absolute Idealist's talk of identity-in-difference at least begins to do justice to the intimacy of the connection. But the proper conclusion to draw, I suggest, is that there is no property, *redness*.

My argument has been that there cannot be any determinable universals: all universals must be determinate. But some philosophers are prepared to question whether there have to be any determinate universals. Things have length, but is there anything which has an absolutely precise length? Every measurement involves a margin of error, which may be reduced but never eliminated. May there not, they ask, be an indeterminacy in the world to correspond to this indeterminacy of measurement? The same argument may be repeated for other quantities, and for ranges of qualities which vary continuously. It may then be claimed that contemporary physics actually gives some support to the thesis that reality can be thus indeterminate.

In considering this position, it is necessary first to draw a distinction. It does seem possible that the notion of length, say, should turn out to be one which is dispensable in fundamental science. Nothing "obeys the law of Newtonian gravitation" because, we now believe, no such law really holds. It is approximately true only. So, it may turn out, there is no such thing as length, but simply appearances of particulars having length, appearances founded upon other, genuine, properties. In that case there will be no absolutely determinate lengths, because there are no lengths at all. A milder possibility would be the breakdown of the notion of length in the regions of what the language of length would call "the very small".

Such possibilities we may admit. Perhaps current physics gives them some support. But should we admit cases where things do have length, indeed, have some reasonably definite length, but, within a certain narrower range of lengths, do not definitely have one length rather than another?

With great hesitation, I am prepared to allow that this *may* be a possibility. But if it is a possibility, then we cannot have a classical logic. Suppose that the length of a certain particular at a certain time is said to be indeterminate over a certain range. It has $L_1$ or $L_2$ or ... But this is not because it has, say, $L_1$, while lacking any other of the disjuncts. Nor is it because the particular has each one of the disjuncts. If we allow this as a possibility, then we require "disjunctive" properties which do not obey the truth-table for classical disjunction.

In ch. 14 it was argued that we ought not to admit (classical) disjunctive properties. Perhaps, however, developments in quantum physics or elsewhere will force the introduction of non-classical disjunctive properties. If so, however, it may still be possible to reconstruct the notions of determinable and determinate. The determinate properties will become, not absolute determinates, but "disjunctive" ranges of determinates. The argument of the next section will in fact proceed in terms of *absolute* determinates, but, if we are forced to, then I think that it should be possible to reconstruct the argument to apply to this revised notion of a determinate.

## 11 *A solution in terms of partial identity*

It will be assumed, then, that to say that *a* is red is to say that *a* has *some* property, a property which is a member of a class of properties, *viz*. the class of the absolutely determinate shades of red. But what constitutes the unity of this class? We have now to attempt an answer.

However, epistemological difficulties make the case of colours a a case of peculiar difficulty. In this section, therefore, the discussion will proceed in terms of the lengths. The solution given for length will then be applied to colour in the next section.

Even in the case of length some simplifying assumptions will be made. It will be assumed, first, that, as a matter of empirical fact, every possible length is an actual length. That is, the Principle of Instantiation is satisfied for each possible length. Second, a Newtonian, that is, pre-Relativistic, account of length will be assumed.

We may start from a point which has already been remarked upon. Resemblance between universals may be more or less close, and the limit of that resemblance is identity. This vital clue was noted by W. E. Johnson (1921, pp. 191–2 and 1922, p. 172) and D. J. O'Connor (1946). The latter wrote:

> The connection [between similarity and identity] is that identity in these cases [simple sense qualities] is the limit of a series which converges in a special way and whose terms consist of pairs of qualities. (p. 55)

How can we explain this convergence to identity? It might be thought that it was a matter of the properties having more and more common properties. If all their properties are the same, they are the same property (the Identity of Indiscernibles holding true for properties). However, in ch. 21 § 11 it was seen that the resemblance of determinate properties falling under a common determinate cannot be explained in terms of common properties.

Whether or not universals have properties, they do, if they are complex, have parts. Philosophers are perfectly familiar with the distinction between the parts of a particular (which are also particulars) and its properties (which are universals). They are less familiar with the distinction between the parts of a universal (which are also universals) and its properties (which are universals of a higher order). But it was argued in ch. 15 § 11 that the notion of a part should not be restricted to particulars, still less to spatial particulars, but was applicable to any complex entity, including complex universals.[1]

If (complex) universals have parts, then they are capable of *partial identity*. One universal may be a part of another or two universals may overlap. If *P&Q* is a conjunctive property, then *P* and *Q* are parts of it. And if *Q&R* is also a property, then it overlaps with *P&Q*.

Partial identity, whether of particulars, universals or anything else there may be, admits of at least rough-and-ready degree. Consider, for instance, larger and larger portions of a cake. Furthermore, partial identity converges to a limit, which is identity. The largest portion of all is the cake itself. Switching from particulars to universals, consider the conjunctive property, *P&Q&R&S*. The properties, *P*, *P&Q*, *P&Q&R*, are all partially identical with this property. What is more, they form a simple series whose limit is identity with *P&Q&R&S*. Again, each successive member of the series may be said to resemble *P&Q&R&S* more closely.

It is, then, a hypothesis well worth examining, that what unifies the class of universals which constitute the class of lengths is a series of partial identities holding between the members of the class.

The model provided by conjunctive properties is a simple one, and so is useful in explaining a relatively unfamiliar, though not really difficult, notion, that of the partial identity of universals. For our purposes here, however, it is a ladder which must now be kicked away. It is impossible that a greater length should stand to a lesser length as conjunctive property to conjunct. For particulars which have the property, *P&Q*, also have the property, *P*. Yet it is

---

[1] The notion of a part of a universal is, of course, to be distinguished from the notion of a part of the aggregate of particulars falling under that universal. To give it that interpretation would only be to demonstrate how deeply one was dominated by the notion that parts are always parts of particulars. Equally, a part of a universal is not a sub-class of the class of particulars falling under that universal. The aggregate of *P&Q*s may actually be a part of the aggregate of *P*s, and the class of *P&Q*s a sub-class of the class of *P*s. Yet *P* is the part, and *P&Q* the whole.

impossible that one particular should, at the one time, have two different lengths.

However, in ch. 15 § II and again in ch. 18 § III it was noted that it is a false principle that the parts of a universal always instantiate the very same particulars as the universal itself. Indeed, we called this false principle the *Conjunction Principle*, because it is only in the case of conjunctive universals that the parts *must* qualify the same particulars as the whole. Suppose that P is a *structural* property, a matter of something which is F standing in the relation R to something which is G (for structural properties, see ch. 18 §§ III and IV). It is not at all necessary that particulars which are P also be F and be G.

It may therefore be suggested that lengths are structural properties and that any lesser length stands to any greater length as proper part to whole.

But at this point a difficulty arises. If we consider *being one metre in length*, and take it to be a structural property, then, among the lesser lengths which it contains will be, for instance, *being one half-metre in length*. But a metre is *two* half-metres. There can, however, be only *one* universal, *being one half-metre in length*.

The problem is solved by realizing that *being one half-metre in length*, like many (perhaps all) structural properties, is a *particularizing* property. It picks out instances which can be said to be unambiguously *one* instance of a particular that is half a metre long. Such a universal is simultaneously a certain *type* of state of affairs: the type *something's being one half-metre in length*.[1]

Particularizing properties give rise to a potentially infinite series of structural properties: in this case *being one half-metre in length, being two half-metres in length . . . . being n half-metres in length. Being a metre in length*, therefore, may be said to contain *being one half-metre in length* and to be equivalent to *being two half-metres in length*. It is in this way that lengths (the universals) contain lesser lengths, that is, stand to the lesser lengths as whole to part. This fact constitutes the unity of the class of lengths.

At the beginning of this chapter, four characteristics of the class of shapes were listed, characteristics which we wished to explain. Let us

---

[1] For states of affairs, see ch. 11 § III. For particularizing properties see ch. 11 § IV and ch. 18 §§ I and III. It may be noted that *being one half-metre in length* is only a *weakly* particularizing property. It does not "divide its instantiations" in the way that *being an electron* does.

now, partly by way of summing up the argument, run through the corresponding characteristics of the lengths.

First, we have to account for what is common to all the lengths. We must explain what makes them all lengths. This is done when we see that any two members of the class of lengths, structural and particularizing universals as they are, stand to each other as whole to part or part to whole. This is a very tight unity indeed. It seems a fair exchange in return for abandoning the idea that there is an identity running through each member of the class.

Second, what the lengths "agree" in, they all differ in. They are all different universals. This feature of the class of lengths we simply accept.

Third, the lengths exhibit a resemblance-order based upon their intrinsic natures. *Being a foot* resembles *being a yard* more than it resembles *being a mile*. This order is explained by the order which holds among the partial identities. It is simply the transitivity of part to whole. The resemblance may be more or less close, because the partial identity may be more or less close to the limiting case of *complete* identity.

Fourth, and finally, the lengths form a set-of-incompatibles. No two lengths can be lengths of exactly the same particular (in respect of the same dimension). This phenomenon is traceable to the fact that the lesser length is a part of the *structural* property which is the greater length. It is in general the case that a part of a structural property does not characterize the very same particulars which the structural property characterizes.

It thus seems fairly simple to explain the special characteristics of the class of the determinate lengths. If the account is correct, or is on the right track, it should not be too difficult to apply it to more complex cases, for instance, the class of the shapes. The ordering principles of the class of the shapes are obviously more complex than those of the class of the lengths. But nothing more than complication seems to be involved. The fundamental notion involved will still be partial identity of the structural properties concerned. However, the partial identities may take the form of overlap as well as whole to part.

Can the solution be said to. be a solution which appeals to relations between universals? Not really, I think. We have argued that identity is not a relation. In the case of partial identity, the completely distinct portions may be said to be related to each other. For instance, if there are two properties, *P&Q* and *Q&R*, the properties, P and R, supposed wholly distinct, may be said to be related to each other. They have the relation of *having a common conjunct*. But this relation can be analysed without invoking anything more than first-order particulars and first-order properties. Here is the analysis. There are particulars, $x$ and $y$, and a property, $\varnothing$, such that $x$ has P and $\varnothing$, and $y$ has R and $\varnothing$.

In the same way, the partial identities which, I have argued, hold together the class of the lengths, and the class of the shapes, do involve what are, in a sense, relations between universals. But they are relations which can be analysed in wholly first-order terms. Surprising as it may seem, these resemblances involve no higher-order universals.

### III *The solution extended to colours*

How is the solution given in the previous section to be transferred from a case like length to the case of colour and other "secondary" qualities? The class of the colours appears to have similar formal characteristics to the class of lengths. But, unlike lengths, colours do not appear to be complex structures. How, then, can the colours be treated in the same way that we have just treated lengths?

Philosophers have often been dominated by the model of "clear and distinct perception". For those dominated by this model, what does not appear complex is not complex. G. F. Stout, for instance, wrote:

> My difficulty is that I cannot by any kind of scrutiny discern any such complexity in any specific red. (1936, p. 14)

In a famous footnote, Hume discusses the resemblance of *blue, green* and *scarlet*. He says:

> It is evident, that even different simple ideas may have a similarity or resemblance to each other; nor is it necessary, that the point or circumstance of resemblance should be distinct or separable from that in which they differ. *Blue* and *green* are different simple ideas, but are more resembling than *blue* or *scarlet*; though their perfect simplicity [*nota bene*] excludes all possibility of separation or distinction. It is the same with particular sounds, and tastes, and smells. These admit of infinite resemblance upon the general

appearance and comparison, without having any common circumstance the same. (*Treatise*, Bk. I Part I § VII)

This fine passage shows exactly why it has often been held that at least some resemblances between universals are a matter of *irreducible* relations. (I am here accepting Church's rather than Hendel's interpretation of this passage. See the last section of the previous chapter.) For both Stout and Hume phenomenology decides the question of ontology. The solution to the problem of the resemblance of *blue, green* and *scarlet* cannot lie in partial identity of the properties involved, because that would demand that the properties be complex when, observably, they are not. Furthermore, rejection of the solution in terms of partial identity here leads to the same solution being largely ignored in the case of the lengths, although in the latter case it is staring straight at us. For the close resemblance of the two problems suggests that, whatever solutions they have, they must have parallel solutions.

I believe, however, that we should not be daunted by the phenomenological difficulties which daunted Stout and Hume. It is useful here to go back to the resemblance of particulars. In ch. 20 § II, we discussed the problem-situation where a resemblance is noted between two particulars, such as faces, but we are unable to make out, even at a sub-verbal and/or unconscious level, any respect of resemblance. We saw that this epistemological or phenomenological fact is compatible with the *ontological* proposition that this resemblance is resemblance in a definite respect. For it does not follow from the fact that resemblance is resemblance in a respect, that recognizing the resemblance involves recognizing the respect.

(1) S recognizes that *a* and *b* resemble each other in some respect
(2) That respect is C
∴ (3) S recognizes that *a* and *b* resemble each other in respect C

is an invalid argument.

May there not be similar phenomena to be encountered in the case of the resemblance of universals? May not the determinate colours be complex properties capable of partial identity with each other? But may it not be that, unlike the case of the lengths, we are not directly aware of the complexity and partial identity of the colours? We grant Stout and Hume that the colours are epistemologically simple. But we maintain that they are ontologically complex. It is then possible to solve the problem of the colours in the same simple way that we solved the problem of the lengths. The properties involved resemble each other because they are partially identical.

In the case of different lengths, one universal contains another. The corresponding ordinary concepts and predicates reflect this fact. The partial identities are in plain view. Of two different lengths (lengths as universals) we can say which contains the other. In the case of the colours and the other secondary qualities, the corresponding ordinary concepts and predicates fail to make the partial identity plain. They do give us hints as to the truth. I have claimed that, as a result of a good deal of difficult philosophical reflection (ch. 21, in particular) we see that the phenomena so ably described by Hume cannot have the character which they appear to have. If the colours really are simple, then they cannot resemble each other in the way that they do. This resemblance can only be explained, I suggest, by their partial identity. Nevertheless, in the case of the colours the partial identity has to be inferred as the result of a difficult argument. If I may so put the matter, in the case of length the partial identity lies much nearer the surface.

What makes it difficult to accept the notion that properties such as the colours are epistemologically simple but ontologically complex is the idea that our grasp of colour is a *total* grasp. Philosophers, especially those sympathetic to the "British Empiricist" tradition, find it hard to banish the notion that we have a *through-and-through* perceptual acquaintance with the qualities. We think that there can be no hidden depths in these qualities to which perception fails to reach.

The source of our error seems to spring from the fantasies of infallibility and omniscience which have bedevilled enquiry generally, and philosophy in particular, from the beginning. Most of us have painfully learnt the lesson which the Phenomenalists have not fully learnt: that the general nature of physical objects is given to us by perception only very imperfectly. But the repressed appetite for infallibility and omnisience then retreats to the universals which the objects instantiate. Among these universals, at any rate for British Empiricists, it settles in particular upon the *perceived* qualities and relations. In fact, however, perceived qualities and relations are as much epistemological icebergs as any other aspect of reality.

If we ask what in fact the colours are, the physicalist reductions of these properties to light-emissions of different wave-length promises to reproduce the required logical characteristics. The differing wave-lengths form a class of structural properties with a similar logical structure to the lengths, if more complex. The incompatibility of colours, and the fact that they exhibit a resemblance-order having as its upper limit complete identity, are then easily explained.

A residual epistemological problem remains. How can we be aware of the resemblance and the incompatibility of the colour-shades, yet be unaware of, and have to infer, the nature of the colour-properties from which these features flow? The answer, I take it, is in principle the same, if more complex in detail, as for the cases where resemblance of particulars such as faces is observed but the respect of resemblance cannot be made out. Despite the fact that the respect in which the faces resemble one another is not identified, it can still act upon our mind, producing in us an awareness of resemblance. In the same way, why should not the colour-properties act on our mind (or, rather, why should not states of affairs involving these properties act on our mind) producing awareness of resemblance and incompatibility, but not producing awareness of those features of the properties from which the resemblance and incompatibility flow?

## IV *Homogeneous classes of universals*

In ch. 21 § III, we examined R. W. Church's view that the unity of classes of determinates, such as the class of colours, depended upon an ordering relation holding between the members of the class. This view is tantalizingly close to the truth. But it implies that the unity of the class is secured by relations between universals (second-order relations). I have asserted, instead, that the unity is secured by partial identities. 'Is a part of' and 'overlaps with' are the two-place predicates which apply to certain universals, such as two lengths, but no relation is involved. The predicates apply simply in virtue of what the universals are.

It is true that wherever universals are partially identical, there are wholly distinct universals which may be said to be related. But such relations can be analysed in purely first-order terms (see the end of § II).

It will be argued in the next Part that there are second-order properties and relations. But I have claimed to give an account of, for example, what it is for *redness* to be a colour or *redness* to resemble *orangeness* more than it resembles *blueness* without appeal to second-order universals. This is somewhat ironic, because it is facts such as these which have often been taken to show that there must be second-order universals.

It may be said that such classes as the class of lengths "form a family". The question then arises what differentiates such classes of universals from, say, the class formed by the different sorts of game. In each case partial identities are involved. What is the difference? It is intuitively obvious that the class of lengths is a much closer-knit family than the class of games. But how can we spell out this difference more exactly?

Select just one member of the class of lengths. All the lesser lengths are structural parts of this length. This length is a structural part of all greater lengths. Assign the number 1 to it. All the lesser and greater lengths may be assigned distinct positive real numbers, numbers which measure the proportion which the lengths bear to length 1. In this fashion, the class of lengths is united by a single, topic-neutral, formula.

Contrast the class of games. Given the properties which make a particular game a game, there is, it seems plausible to say, no single, topic-neutral, formula from which all and only the other species of game can be derived. There is no substitute for knowing the many different sorts of game which just happen to mark out the boundaries of the class of game-types.

Colours are a controversial case. Granting the physicalist reduction of determinate shades of colour to mixtures of light of a certain wave-length, it is unclear whether, for each shade, there is a genuinely unitary formula for the mixtures associated with each shade. Again, it is unclear whether the colour-circle can be unified by a genuine unitary formula in the way that the lengths can be unified (see Keith Campbell, 1969).

In ch. 13 § IV, a classification of predicates which are both "pure" (applying solely in virtue of universals) and "open" was proposed. The classification was in terms of degree, the highest degree being that where a predicate applied solely in virtue of a single universal. Predicates of the next degree were called "homogeneous" predicates, and 'having length' and 'having mass' were suggested as examples. We can now see a bit more clearly the nature of the classes of universals in virtue of which such predicates apply. They are classes of partially identical universals, but where the class is unified by a topic-neutral formula of the sort illustrated in the case of the lengths. We may call the classes "homogeneous classes" of universals.

Below homogeneous predicates are to be found "family" predicates. Here there are still partial identities, but there is no unifying formula. Below these again are "heterogeneous" predicates, such predicates as 'either a raven or a writing-desk', where the predicates do not even apply in virtue of disorganized partial identities.

### v *The Laws of Nature as linking homogeneous classes of universals*

The nature of nomic or law-like connection is a topic for ch. 24. Here I am simply concerned to point out that it is not, in general, simple universals which are nomically linked, but rather homogeneous classes of universals, such as the class of lengths or of masses.

It is possible to have nomic necessities with the simple form 'for all $x$, if $x$ is F, then $x$ is G' where F and G are genuine properties. An example may be the law that every electron has charge $e$. But what we are more likely to find is a functional correlation or, as Mill put it, a concomitant variation, between homogeneous classes of universals. The paradigm of such a class is that "generated" by a continuously varying quantity.

Such a homogeneous class of universals, when it is nomically correlated with another homogeneous class, has a claim to be called a "natural" class of universals. Such classes are of much greater moment in scientific theory than single universals. That is why 'strictly universal predicates', although they have been very important for our argument, are not so important for the theory of science.

The simplest case of nomic correlation of homogeneous classes of universals will be that where two classes of properties are linked by a function such that, given that a particular has a property which is a certain member of the first class, then it is nomically determined that *that particular* will also have a certain definite property belonging to the second class. Given that the volume is such, then the temperature must be such and such. Obviously, however, this will be something of a limiting case. Homogeneous classes of universals may be, and are, nomically correlated in much more complex and sophisticated ways than this. But even with the simple correlation of the sort just described we have something which looks more like the laws actually proposed by scientists, especially in the fundamental science of physics, than the jejune formula: (x) (Fx ⊃ Gx).

Nomic correlations of homogeneous classes of universals allow the possibility of making and justifying rather sophisticated counter-factual claims. It may be the case that a certain member of such a class of universals is not instantiated (at any time). Hume's "missing shade of blue" is an imaginary example. Given the Principle of Instantiation it follows that there is no such universal, only the concept of such a universal. But on the basis of the nomic correlations of the classes involved we could formulate and justify counter-factuals. We could say, for instance, that *if* that universal were in-stantiated, then such instances would have such and such a further property.

## vi *Predicates and universals again*

The view that there are no determinable universals, but only deter-minates, has important semantic and epistemological consequences. I will end this chapter by a brief mention of two of these. I tie my discussion to some interesting remarks by the late Everett W. Hall (1957). He wrote:

> Suppose I say, "My pen is grey" the subject, 'my pen', uniquely refers to a particular, not by naming it directly but by indirect reference via another particular (me) which is directly referred to. But 'grey' is not a name, or a definite description, nor any device for unique reference to a single universal. The colour appears am-biguously; it is not specified which grey, of a large variety of dis-cernible ones, is being spoken of. 'Grey' is here short for 'greyish' or 'of a greyish hue' [of some determinate shade of grey]. This is a case of indefinite reference just as truly as 'a pen' in 'there is a pen on the table'. (p. 479)

Hall offers two explanations of this indefiniteness. First, he says:

> Most of our day-to-day speech is not at all concerned to pinpoint the universal it is attributing to some particular; rather it appears entirely satisfied with a vague indication of a region or set of universals in which the one involved falls, for our interest in just that one is short-lived. (p. 479)

I agree with Hall that such a factor is often responsible for the inexactness of our predicates. The exactness of our non-verbal apprehension of a property often exceeds the exactness of the predicate used. This may be due to poverty of linguistic resources. Again, it may be due to the economic advantage of making our descriptions less precise than we could have made them if we had put more effort into them. ('Near enough is good enough', as the Australians say.) Finally, it may be due to sheer carelessness and inattention.

Second, Hall mentions a factor which he plays down, but which I think is even more important than the factor he emphasizes. He says:

> I do not wish to exclude the possibility that we sometimes experience universals indeterminately and not merely refer to them anonymously. (p. 480)

I would say, more strongly, that for almost all universals (perhaps all) we *experience* them indeterminately. The universal itself, we have asserted, is absolutely determinate, with the reservation that it may be necessary to admit non-classical disjunctive properties (see § 1). But our powers of perception, and of discrimination generally, fall short of the absolutely determinate. Particulars are not perceived as having a certain absolute determinate nature, but instead as falling within a certain range of universals. Furthermore, our predicates will, in general, follow our experience and so they, too, will not be absolutely determinate.

# PART SEVEN

# HIGHER-ORDER UNIVERSALS

# 23

## *Higher-order properties*

I come finally to what is perhaps the most difficult and obscure part of this enquiry.

Particulars have properties and stand in relations. But do these properties and relations in turn have their own properties and relations? More succinctly: "Are there second-order universals?" And if so, are there universals of still higher order? It is obvious, of course, that numerous one- and many-place predicates apply to properties and relations. But do these predicates apply in virtue of genuine properties and relations of these properties and relations?

If there are higher-order universals, then it is necessary also to introduce the notion of different orders of particulars. What we have up to this point for the most part simply called "particulars" will become "first-order particulars". They are the absolute particulars. The properties and relations of these particulars are "first-order" universals. But suppose that these universals themselves fall under monadic universals (properties) and polyadic universals (relations). The new properties and relations will be "second-order" universals. Furthermore, the first-order universals will simultaneously be "second-order particulars": for they are particulars relative to *their* universals. And so on up the scale.

I shall be arguing that there are in fact higher-order universals. Bergmann and his followers call the claim that there are no such universals the thesis of "Elementarism" (see, for instance, Bergmann, 1957). So I shall be rejecting Elementarism. It has to be said, however, that hitherto the theory of higher-order universals, to the extent that it has existed, has been practically a Rationalist enclave. It has almost invariably been assumed that, if there are higher-order universals, their existence can be determined *a priori*

simply on the basis of knowing what first-order universals there
are.[1]

John Anderson was an exception, although he might have objected at least to the terminology of "higher-order" universals.
What we must now try to develop is an Empiricist theory of higher-
order universals.

### 1 Second-order properties

I begin by asking whether first-order universals ever have properties, and, if so, of what sort. I restrict the term "properties" here for
the present to non-relational properties.

Let us begin by collecting possible examples of such properties.
A natural way to proceed is to consider what one-place, but apparently non-relational, predicates are applied to first-order universals.
We know that predicates do not guarantee properties. But we also
know that such predicates will give us the best first clue which we
have to the properties, if there are any, of those universals.

Given a first-order property or relation, then, such one-place
predicates as 'property', 'relation', 'simple', 'complex', 'homoeomerous', 'anomoeomerous', 'asymmetrical', 'being a colour',
'having just two instances', 'existing in just such-and-such a quantity' apply to some of these properties and relations. They do not
appear to apply in virtue of relations that these universals have to
further objects. So perhaps some at least of these predicates apply in
virtue of properties of the universals.

Many philosophers have taken it that statements like 'Red is a
colour' attribute a property to a property. And even if, as has been
argued in ch. 22 § 1, 'red' is a predicate which applies not in virtue
of a single property but rather in virtue of a disjunctive range of
properties, it might still be the case that *being a colour* is a property
of each member of this range. However, as we have also argued in
that section, if *being a colour* is a genuine property of the determinate shades of red, then it would have to be the case that each
shade was *identical* in that respect. *Being a colour* would have to be
genuinely a one which ran through the many. It was, however,
argued further that *being a colour* does not meet this condition.

[1] Butchvarov (1966, p. 176) writes:
   "If there are universals, our knowledge of their relations would appear to be *a
   priori*, and the propositions describing these relations, necessary."
   Plato's Hierarchy of Forms is the first (the first Rationalist) theory of higher-order
   universals.

Hence, although *being a colour* is often offered as a paradigm of a second-order property, we cannot accept that it is in fact such a property. As was argued in the previous chapter, the unity of the class of colours is secured in another way.

What of other predicates in our list? Suppose that all the statements about first-order universals in which these predicates occur could be wholly *analysed* in terms of statements attributing first-order universals to first-order particulars. Then we would get the best of both worlds. The situation would be the same as that with (first-order) relational properties. Such properties are real but onto-logically they are nothing over and above the relations and (non-relational) properties of particulars (ch. 19 § 11). In the same fashion, the properties of universals would be real, but would involve no higher-order universals. The thesis of Elementarism would be true (at least with respect to *properties* of first-order universals).

This seems to be the case with some of our predicates. 'Having just two instances' is a case in point. *Having just two instances* appears to be a respect in which (particularizing) universals can be identical. If the predicate is applicable to a property, P, then, in familiar fashion, we can say that there exists a first-order particular, $x$, such that $x$ is P, and a particular, $y$, such that $x \neq y$ and such that $y$ is P, and that for all first-order particulars, $z$, if $z$ is P, $z = x$ or $z = y$. Similarly, at greater length, for all attribution of a finite number of instances. No appeal to higher-order properties of P is involved. Other reductive analyses may be possible in the case of 'having an infinite number of instances' (for various infinite numbers) and 'existing in such-and-such a quantity'.

However, I think that there are properties on our list for which the thesis of Elementarism fails. As an example, consider the predicate 'complex' as applied to a property.

(1) Property, P, is complex

cannot be analysed as:

(2) For all particulars, x, if x is P, then x is complex in nature.

For while (2) is undoubtedly entailed by (1), a type of entailment of great importance which will be discussed shortly, (2) does not entail (1). For P might be simple, yet all particulars which were P be complex in nature, provided only that all such particulars had other properties, simple or complex, besides P.

This stands in sharp contrast to:

(1′) Relation R is transitive.

This entails that:

(2′) For all particulars, x, y and z, if xRy and yRz, then xRz.

But not only does (1′) entail (2′), (2′) also entails (1′). It may therefore be denied that a transitive relation has the irreducible, or second-order, property of *being transitive*. An Elementarist analysis of (1′), *viz*. (2′), is available.

It is useless to alter (2) to:

(3) *Necessarily*, for all particulars, x, if x is P, then x is complex in nature.

For what would make this a necessary truth? It would be necessary if, given the existence of P, it was also given that P is complex. But unless a property is specified as complex, it is not a necessary truth that it is complex.

A better attempt, perhaps, is:

(4) For all particulars, x, if x is P, and if there does not exist a property, Q, wholly distinct from P, such that x is Q, then x is complex in nature.

This says that particulars which have property, P, and nothing more than that property, are complex in nature.

The translation is, however, a strange one. For the property, P, although complex, may be one which, by itself, is incapable of being the whole nature of a particular. For instance, P might be a determinate length or a determinate mass, and it does not seem possible that a first-order particular should have a determinate length, or a determinate mass, and no other property whatsoever. In such cases it could only be said that if, *per impossibile*, a particular had P, and P alone, then the particular would be complex in nature. This suggests very strongly that it is *the complexity of P* which explains the complexity of nature of particulars which are P, and that (4) is not a reductive analysis of that complexity. I can find no other more satisfactory translation, so I conclude that (1) cannot be analysed in first-order terms.

Once it is granted that 'P is complex' cannot be analysed in purely first-order terms, then it seems that we must admit that *being complex* is a genuine second-order property of universals. The class of complex universals is an open class: there is no upper limit to the number of complex universals. Again, complexity appears to be something which is *identical* in every complex universal.

If *being complex* is a genuine second-order property of universals, then it seems that *being simple* is not a (possible) second-order property. For *being simple* is *not being complex*, and it was argued in ch. 14 § 11, that the absence of a genuine property is not a property. However, this argument shows at best that one of the two is not really a property. Why is *being complex* given the preference?

I offer two arguments, though I do not claim that they are conclusive. We have already noted that:

(1)  Property, P, is complex

entails

(2)  For all particulars, x, if x is P, then x is complex in nature. However, it is obvious that:

(1″)  Property, Q, is simple

does not entail

(2″)  For all particulars, x, if x is Q, then x is simple in nature.

Indeed, no entailment of any interest can be obtained from (1″).

I call the argument from (1) to (2) a case of "the descent to first-order particulars". I suggest that it is always present where there is a genuine higher-order property or (as we shall see in the next chapter) higher-order relation. If this is accepted, then *being simple* is not a genuine second-order property.

The second argument for saying that *being complex* is a genuine property while *being simple* is not turns on the fact that the complexity of a property can be naturally linked with the causal powers that the property bestows in a way that the simplicity of a property cannot be. Further development of this argument must be postponed for a little while.

If this argument is correct, then we are in a position to criticize as unsound an argument of Hume's. In the footnote (*Treatise*, Bk. 1 Part 1 § vii) where he argues that *blue, green* and *scarlet* are perfectly simple, have no "common circumstance" the same, yet resemble each other, he goes on:

> And of this we may be certain, even from the very abstract terms *simple idea.* They comprehend all simple ideas under them. These resemble each other in their simplicity. And yet from their very nature, which excludes all compositon, this circumstance in which they resemble, is not distinguishable or separable from the rest.

But if simplicity is not a property, we can deny that simple things resemble each other in respect of their simplicity. The predicate 'simple', that is 'not complex', attaches to all simple things, if there are any, but this is not sufficient for resemblance.

Unlike, say, the putative higher-order property *being a colour, being complex* is a formal or topic-neutral property. (I do not know how to define the notion of a formal or topic-neutral property, but I trust it is reasonably clear intuitively. Purely logical, mathematical and mereological notions are my paradigms, and are perhaps the only cases which should be admitted.) This leads me to advance a principle, which may be called the *Formalist* Principle:

> All higher-order properties are formal properties.

This, however, is a restricted version of the Formalist Principle. The unrestricted version, which I am also inclined to defend but which is relevant to the next chapter only, is:

> All higher-order universals are formal universals.

I begin the defence of the Formalist Principle (which I put forward in a tentative spirit) by considering a very different thesis: that every universal is wholly determined by its properties. This view leads to an infinite regress, because the higher-order properties would then require properties of still higher order, and so on. The regress appears to be vicious: we never reach properties which actually determine the nature of any universal. In any case, it is absurdly uneconomical. Furthermore, the establishing of the existence of infinite hierarchies of universals by *a priori* reasoning is utterly in conflict with the principles of *a posteriori* Realism.

It seems, then, that at some point in the regress of higher-order properties we must reach properties which do not themselves have properties but simply are their own unique selves. This uniqueness cannot be a universal because, by hypothesis, it is not a one which can run through many. (Abner Shimony's interesting but excessively Rationalist-oriented discussion of higher-order universals, 1948, appears not to appreciate this last point.)

Of course, though, the argument of the last two paragraphs is very far from establishing the Formalist Principle that the properties of universals are confined to formal or topic-neutral properties. And it might be thought that there are plausible actual examples of non-formal properties of universals: for instance, the intensity or saturation of colours.

Here, then, is a general argument purporting to show that there cannot be, or at least there cannot be any reason to postulate, non-formal properties of universals. It was argued in ch. 16 § 1 that if there is to be any reason to postulate a universal, then it must endow the particulars which instantiate it with causal powers differing from the powers bestowed by another universal. The totality of powers bestowed by a universal must be unique. A second-order but non-formal property of a first-order universal, if there is to be any reason to postulate it, must therefore make its special contribution to the unique set of powers bestowed by the first-order universal. The problem is then to identify just what that special contribution is.

It might be thought that the job could be done in the following way. The alleged second-order property will be common to a number of first-order universals. Each of these universals will bestow its own special powers upon first-order particulars. But the unique sets of powers will presumably involve overlaps. There may well be a sub-set of each of these sets which is common and peculiar to the sets. The second-order property might then be held responsible for this common and peculiar factor.

However, this attempted solution of the problem faces great conceptual difficulties. The hypothesis that a second-order property makes a certain contribution to the causal powers bestowed by its particulars (first-order universals) upon first-order particulars is logically impossible to test experimentally. In particular, the Method of Difference could not be applied. To apply that Method, we would have to *detach* the second-order property from its particulars, the first-order universals. If the first-order universals which had been reduced to this wounded state then failed to bestow certain powers on first-order particulars which they normally did bestow, these missing powers could be confidently attributed to the missing second-order property. However, such detachment is logically impossible. If property, P, has some non-formal property, P', then it must be the case that it has P' in each instance of P. Only if we held a Particularist theory of properties, which we have claimed to refute in ch. 8, could we make any sense of the detachment of second-order properties.

But if a hypothesis is one which it is logically impossible ever to test experimentally, then it cannot be taken very seriously by a scientific Realism about universals. I do not claim that this argument is conclusive. But I do think that it gives a strong reason for not postulating non-formal second-order properties.

However, I have claimed that first-order universals can have formal or topic-neutral second-order properties. Do not formal properties face the same difficulty which has just been spelled out for non-formal second-order properties? I suggest not. Consider, as an example of a formal property, *being conjunctive*. Suppose that P is a conjunctive property, the conjuncts being in fact Q and R. P's *conjunctivity* appears to be a second-order property of P. Certainly, any first-order analysis seems to be unavailable. (*Having Q as conjunct* and *having R as conjunct* are not properties of P. See § III.) At the same time, there is "descent to first-order particulars": particulars which are P must have at least two properties. By the Principle of Instantiation, there must be particulars which are P. Furthermore, there may be particulars which are Q but not R, and others which are R but not Q. This makes it at the very least logically possible to determine the causal "weight" of P, of Q without R, and of R without Q, three "weights" which will all be different. If we have a good theory from which it follows that an object having *both* Q and R will bestow just the powers that P in fact bestows, then we have good reason to think that P *is* the conjunction of Q and R. So we can conclude that P has the property of *being conjunctive*.

Admittedly, if Q and R are nomically co-extensive, so that, of nomic necessity, for all $x$, $x$ is Q if and only if $x$ is R, then there will be no reason to think that P is conjunctive. But that is just to say that we have no reason to postulate conjunctive properties where there is nomic co-extensiveness, that is, under the circumstances we have no reason to postulate a certain sort of formal second-order property. This can simply be accepted.

I believe that the argument here developed in the case of the property of conjunctivity can be repeated, *mutatis mutandis*, in the case of other formal second-order properties. Structural properties, for instance, appear to have the property, *being structured*. Now it will always be possible in principle to discover that some first-order property has this property. Structural properties involve distinct particulars (distinct parts) with certain properties, these particulars perhaps standing in certain relations to each other. The possession of those properties by these different particulars will be distinct states of affairs. The states of affairs can then play a distinct causal role. Even if the states of affairs involve tokens of the same type, that is, different particulars having the very same property, the particulars will differ in spatio-temporal position, and so may be distinguished in their causal operations. A good theory would then enable us to reconstruct the causal powers of the alleged structural property from the causal powers of its constituents. If the alleged property has these powers, it may confidently be identified as having such-and-such a structure (not itself a property – see § III) and so as having the property of *being structured*.

It may now be noted that it does *not* seem possible to develop an argument of this sort in the case of the putative second-order property, *being simple*. This is the second argument for denying that it really is a property.

There will be special difficulties with such possible second-order properties as *being infinitely complex*. How can a first-order universal be shown to have such a second-order property? But there are also special difficulties about claims that there are an infinite number of first-order particulars of a certain sort, for instance, that there are an infinite number of stars. I think that in both cases the difficulties spring from epistemological puzzles which surround the notion of infinity, and not from the distinction between first- and second-order universals.

## II *The Principle of Order Invariance*

Given that we admit higher-order properties (but only formal ones) Tim Oakley has raised the interesting question whether a universal which is, say, of the second order, having first-order universals as particulars, can also have first-order particulars as particulars. We might be tempted to put forward a Principle of Order Invariance, similar to the Principle of Instantial Invariance briefly argued for in ch. 19 § VII. According to the latter principle if a universal is $n$-adic in one instantiation, then it is $n$-adic in all its instantiations, for all $n$. It cannot be dyadic upon one occasion, triadic upon another. The Principle of Order Invariance would hold that if a universal has particulars of *order* N in one instantiation, then its particulars are of order N in all its instantiations, for all N. It cannot be second-order upon one occasion, first-order upon another.

Perhaps the Principle of Order Invariance is true, but I do not find it so attractive as the Principle of Instantial Invariance. There seem to be *prima facie* counter-examples which are difficult to dispose of. *Having just M parts*, where M is determinate, for instance, seems to be a potential property both of first-order particulars and of first-order universals. I cannot see any reason to deny that there is identity of property here.

For the particular case of *polyadic* universals, that is, relations, we can distinguish between a Strong and a Weak form of the Principle of Order Invariance. The Weak Principle may be formulated thus:

> If there are a number of particulars, and a relation which relates them, then each particular is a particular of the same order.

The Weak Principle is vacuously satisfied for the case of monadic universals. It is weaker than the original Principle because we could accept the Weak Principle and yet hold that there are relations which, in one instantiation, relate particulars all of order N and, in another instantiation, particulars all of a different order, M. If the Strong Principle is true, then all the particulars in the field of a relation are of the same order. With the Weak Principle, this condition is dropped.

The Weak Principle is intuitively much more plausible than the Strong Principle. Plato, in effect, appeals to the Weak Principle in the *Parmenides*, 133a–135a, when he asks how it is possible that the relation of knowledge, or any other relation, should hold between those objects of different order: first-order particulars and Forms. In the realm of the Forms, the Master is master to the Slave; in the realm of particulars, individual masters are masters to individual slaves; but no such relation holds between the Master and individual slaves or between the Slave and individual masters.

It is clear that there can be many-place *predicates* which apply to ordered $n$-tuples, where the members of the $n$-tuple include particulars of different orders. But, although I do not know how to argue for the proposition, I incline to the view that no relations ever correspond to these predicates.

### III *Do second-order properties have properties?*

I am far from thinking that the defence of the Formalist Principle is complete but it is the best that I have been able to achieve. The Weak Principle of Order Invariance I have not defended at all, but have simply appealed to the authority of Plato. I now turn to the question whether second-order properties have any properties themselves. If they have any, then, by the same line of argument employed in the previous section, the properties they have will be formal. But do they have any? I shall argue that they do not.

Investigation of the problem can conveniently begin by considering a troublesome difficulty. It concerns the (apparent) second-order property, *being a property*, possessed by all first-order properties. If we allow this second-order property, then it seems that it, too, will have the property, *being a property*. A dilemma then follows. Either this second-order property is an instance of itself, or else its new property, *being a property*, is the property, *being a second-order property*, which in turn has the property, *being a third-order property*, and so *ad infinitum*. The difficulty about these alternatives is that, whichever is true, it is presumably a truth which can be determined *a priori*. This offends against the principle that it is an *a posteriori* question what properties and relations particulars have, even particulars of second and higher orders.

The same problem arises with the apparent property, *being a universal*. This seems to have the property, *being a universal*, and a similar dilemma ensues.

Let us consider first the dilemma about *being a property*. The second horn seems preferable, despite the alarming proliferation of universals which it threatens. In ch. 19 § VI, we rejected the view that there can be states of affairs having the form Raa. In consistency, it seems that we must deny states of affairs of the form R(P, P), where R is a higher-order relation relating a property (or a relation) to itself. But if we reject R(P, P) we must surely also reject P(P) which is simply the monadic case. (Its "possibility" does not arise at the level of first-order particulars.) But the assertion that *being a property* is a property of itself has the form P(P). I therefore turn away from the first horn.

So let us attack the second horn. Let us grant that al first-order properties have the (formal or topic-neutral) property, *being a first-order property*. It must also be granted that the predicate 'second-order property' applies to this property. But not all one-place predicates apply in virtue of properties. Let us try denying that this predicate applies in virtue of a property, *being a second-order property*. If this denial could be made good, the dilemma would be rebutted.

But is not cutting off the regress at the second-order property, *being a first-order property*, an arbitrary step? Perhaps not. It would not be arbitrary if we had reason to think that no second-order properties had properties. (I do not say "second-order universals" here, because I think that there may be properties of second-order relations. See ch. 24 § III.)

I believe that there is in fact reason to think that no second-order properties have properties. Consider the first-order universals. Now consider their properties, the second-order properties. By the Formalist Principle, all of these will be formal or topic-neutral. The set of second-order properties may not include every possible second-order property because here, as elsewhere, only instantiated properties are admitted. (Suppose, for instance, that no first-order universals are infinitely complex. There will then be no second-order property, *being infinitely complex*.)

Suppose, however, that the set of second-order properties is given (pleonastically, the set of actually instantiated second-order properties). Now suppose further that we were to allow (formal) properties of the second-order properties. It seems that what third- (and higher-) order properties there are would be logically necessitated by what second-order properties there are. The third- and higher-order properties would be deductively accessible from the second-order properties.

What I have just said is really only a generalization of the original problem about *being a first-order property*. But, given *a posteriori* Realism, this widening of the scope of the problem will encourage us to do one of two things. First, we might reject the thesis that there are *any* second-order properties. However, for the reasons given in the previous section, I find it difficult to deny that there are some (formal) second-order properties. The second alternative, to which I incline, is to admit such properties, but deny that they in turn fall under still higher-order properties. Various predicates apply to second-order properties, but not in virtue of properties which they have.

It is true that this attempted way out leaves us with a small-scale version of the problem which faces the Nominalist. What is the basis for the application of the predicates which apply to second-order properties? However, here as elsewhere, a problem which is insoluble on the large scale may be soluble on the small. If, for instance, the properties apparently attributed by the predicate stand to second-order properties as *determinables* to *determinates*, then we seem to be out of the wood. For it was argued in ch. 22 that there are no determinable properties, but simply classes of determinate properties, classes united by a series of partial identities.

An interesting example of a pseudo-property at the level of second-order properties is *being a universal*. This seems to be a determinable having as its determinates *being a monadic universal*, *being a dyadic universal* and so on. (Given the Principle of Instantial Invariance, *q.v.* ch. 19 § vii, no universal can be characterized by more than one of these apparent determinates.) If so, *being a universal* is not really a one which runs through this many. If it is not a second-order property, then the problem whether it itself has the property, *being a universal*, automatically disappears.

I do not know whether all apparent properties of second-order properties can, like the apparent second-order property, *being a universal*, be shown to be determinates. Even if this is not possible, there may be other ways of giving an account of the applicability of one-place predicates to second-order properties. But for good or for ill, I propose that second-order properties lack properties.

Even so, it may still be thought that *a posteriori* Realism faces a problem about the second-order property, *being a property*. For, it may be objected, we know *a priori* of any first-order property that it is a property.

However, I think that this objection is incorrect. Of course we know *a priori* that if something is a property, then it is a property. But this gives no *a priori* knowledge in particular cases. Given that a predicate applies to particulars in virtue of a universal or range of universals, we can still be in the dark as to whether the universals involved are (non-relational) properties of the particular or are instead relations which it has to other particulars. Nor need our ignorance be due simply to a failure to reach a correct logical analysis of the predicate. It might require an empirical investigation to determine whether a certain recognizable feature of a particular was, on the one hand, a property or, on the other, a relation to further particulars.

These remarks apply even to the more general category of *universals*. Even where we know that a predicate applies to a particular, do we always know that it applies or does not apply in virtue of a universal or range of universals? In other terminology, do we always know whether or not a predicate is a *pure* predicate? After logical analysis of the predicate has done all that it can do, we may still be ignorant upon this point. (In any case, as noted above, *being a universal* is a mere determinable.)

Summing up: two main theses have been defended in this chapter. First, the thesis of Formalism with respect to higher-order properties: that they are all formal or topic-neutral, as opposed to "material" properties. Second, that though first-order universals have (formal) properties, these properties lack properties themselves.

I am conscious of the limitations of my arguments for these theses. But perhaps hypotheses, however ill-supported, are of value in such ill-charted territory. I hope that I can do somewhat better in the discussion of what I take to be a much more important topic: *relations* between first-order universals.

## IV *Higher-order relational properties*

Before going on to the next chapter, however, a word about higher-order *relational properties*. In ch. 19 § II, it was argued that first-order relational properties, although real, can be analysed in terms of the non-relational properties, and the relations, of first-order particulars. *Mutatis mutandis*, the same holds for higher-order relational properties. Nevertheless, it will be advisable to discuss certain points in connection with the latter.

Suppose that a first-order universal has a certain relation to another first-order universal. (What the nature of this relation could be is the main business of the next chapter.) $U_1$ has R to $U_2$. Should we say that *having R to $U_2$* is a relational property of $U_1$? Here we must be careful. Go back to the distinction drawn in ch. 13 § IV between impure and pure predicates. 'Descended from Charlemagne' is an impure predicate. It applies to a certain "open" class of particulars in virtue of certain relations which hold between them and a certain other particular: the first Holy Roman Emperor.

'Descended from kings' is, however, a pure predicate. It is utterly unlikely that *being descended from kings* is a genuine relational property. But the predicate applies solely in virtue of universals: genuine, if various, properties and relations in virtue of which the predicate applies.

Now, 'having R to $U_2$' is an *impure* predicate. For $U_2$, although a first-order universal, is also a second-order particular, and to apply this predicate to $U_1$ is to assert that $U_1$ has a certain relation to this second-order particular. *Being descended from Charlemagne* is a matter of relations to just one particular. Similarly, *having R to $U_2$* is a matter of a relation to just one (second-order) particular, a relation which $U_1$, and perhaps other second-order particulars, have to $U_2$.

Hence, given the way in which we have restricted the meaning of the terms "property" and "relation" in this work, *having R to $U_2$* is not a property of $U_1$, not even a relational property. To get a relational *property* we need at least a second-order equivalent of *being descended from kings: viz.* having R to a member of some "open" class of first-order universals.

All this is unchanged if $U_2$ is itself a (genuine) first-order relational property – say, *having S to an F*. $U_1$ might have R to this $U_2$, but *having R to (having S to an F)* is still not a genuine relational property of $U_1$. For S and F are (second-order) particulars. These subtleties will be found relevant to the discussions of the next chapter.

It should be noted also, as was mentioned in § 1, that if P is a conjunctive property, and Q and R are its conjuncts, then *having Q as a conjunct* is not a genuine property of P. In the light of the remarks just made above, it is easy to see that 'having Q as a conjunct' is an *impure* predicate.

# 24

## *Higher-order relations*

This last topic of the book is by no means the least. In some ways, indeed, it is the key-stone of the arch. It not merely completes the structure but binds it together. I shall argue that first-order universals may be related by second-order relations. The all-important notions of causality and nomic connection are to be analysed in terms of these second-order relations. It will be argued further, briefly, that, unlike second-order properties, second-order relations may (though they may not) themselves have properties.

### i *Causality and nomic connection*

Let us consider the relation of causality. Can this relation, or can it not, be analysed without appealing to universals of higher-order? The same question may be asked about nomic connection.

The Humean tradition of thought about causality and nomic connection may be seen as an attempt to give a first-order (Elementarist) analysis of these relations. No second-order relations between properties are required. (A Humean may, although he need not, go further and try to give some Nominalist, that is, reductive, account of properties. This, of course, makes his task still harder.) For simplicity's sake, let us for the present restrict ourselves to *general* causal and nomic connections (e.g. 'Arsenic causes death'). The Humean attempt takes the form of producing unrestricted universally quantified propositions about first-order particulars (whether these are things, events or states of affairs is currently unimportant to us), propositions which are claimed to be analyses of causal and nomic propositions. Just *exactly* what form the analysing propositions are to have is an uncertain matter, a matter for debate among Humeans. For it is very difficult to find Humean analyses which can even give the appearance of being satisfactory. Note, though, that the proponent of a Humean analysis, at least if he is a Realist about universals, need not deny himself variables which range over properties and relations as well as first-order particulars. (He can treat the so-called "higher-order" predicate calculus with ontological seriousness.) All the Humean need deny is that causation and nomic connection require the postulation of relations between the first-order universals.

I believe that, valuable as the attempt was, the Humean programme is a failure. The problem of counter-factuals, in particular, is a notorious scandal for the programme. Statements of causal connection and of laws of nature appear to sustain counter-factual statements in a way that mere unrestricted universally quantified statements do not. Enormous ingenuity has been devoted to the attempt to close the gap, but I judge that this ingenuity has been wasted. In any case, at the level of mere intuition, "constant conjunction" is a completely inadequate account of the majestic and terrible necessity of cause and natural law.

I propose, therefore, that we try to give an account of causal and nomic connection in terms of *second-order* relations: irreducible relations between first-order universals. Two theses are involved. First, causal connection is reducible to nomic connection. Second, in nomic connection one universal necessitates another. *F-ness* necessitates *G-ness*, or *being F* necessitates *being G*. Or *being an F* (a particularizing universal) necessitates *being another F*. (This necessitation must not be identified with logical necessitation.)

First, the link between causation and law. This is not very controversial. It does seem to be an insight of the Humean view that causal connection is a form of law-like connection. It preserves the commonsense insight that certain sorts of cause, working in certain sorts of circumstance, produce only certain sorts of effect. The only view of causality which denies this link between cause and law is the Singularist view which holds that what causes what in one particular situation has no logical bearing upon what causes what in another. (A brief discussion of Singularism is held in ch. 2 § VI.) It is true, of course, that even where we recognize that a certain sequence is a causal one, the description of the sequence which we are able to give is likely not to yield any law-like statement covering the sequence in question. This point was perhaps not clear to Hume, but it is clear to the sophisticated latter-day Humeans. All that need be true is that *there exist* some law-like connection, not necessarily known to anybody, which the sequence instantiates. It is difficult to deny that causal sequences involve law-like connections in this sense.

So we agree that causation involves law-like connection. But what of law-like connection itself? Is this a matter of second-order relations? This point is much more controversial. However, after coming to the view that such relations are indeed involved, I was greatly heartened to discover that Michael Tooley had independently arrived at a very similar view (Tooley, 1977). Still more interestingly, he arrived at it from a different direction, not as a result of thinking about universals, but as a result of thinking about the nature of laws.

Tooley rests great weight upon the following imaginary case. Suppose that there are ten, and only ten, different sorts of fundamental particle in the universe. Suppose that the interactions of any two sorts of particle (including the interactions of a particle with a "twin") are governed by distinct and mutually irreducible laws. There can be no more general law(s) of which these laws are specifications. This gives fifty-five possible sets of irreducible interaction-laws. But only fifty-four sets are known. This is because the boundary-conditions in the universe are such that there is never, at any time, any meeting between particles of type A and type J. There is no nomic difficulty involved. It is just that particles of these two types never happen to meet.

In this situation, Tooley argues, we would have very good reason to believe that there is a definite, unique, irreducible but totally unknown set of laws governing the interactions of an A-type particle with a J-type particle. The existence of the other fifty-four sets of laws is excellent inductive reason for believing that there is a fifty-fifth set. But it is clear that we cannot know the nature of this set of laws.

Tooley argues that no Humean view of laws, however sophisticated, can give an account of this case. For a Humean would be forced to say it was impossible that, in such circumstances, there should be such a set of determinate but unknown laws. A Tooley-like case has also been proposed independently by C. B. Martin. But, as Tooley sees the matter, refutation of Humeanism is far from exhausting the interest of the case. He asks us to consider what is the ontological ground, the truth-maker, for the unknown propositions which assert the existence of the fifty-fifth set of laws. The only plausible truth-maker available, he points out, is the *properties* (conceived of as universals) which make A-type and J-type particles the type of particles they are, together with the *relations* (also universals) which, if they obtained between tokens of these two types of particle, would, we believe, trigger off the special type of interaction, an interaction which itself would involve various properties and relations. He draws the conclusion that the unknown laws themselves can only be (second-order) *relations* between these first-order properties and relations.

I believe that with this case Tooley has provided powerful support for the view that laws of nature are relations of universals. At the same time, however, the case raises awkward problems for the particular view of laws of nature which I wish to uphold. The laws in Tooley's case would be *uninstantiated* laws, and there would be no "descent to first-order particulars", thus offending against the Principle of Instantiation. So for the present I will leave such cases as Tooley's aside. After my view has been developed further I will suggest an analysis of Tooley's case.

It is clear, at any rate, that Realism about universals is a *necessary* condition for solving the cause/law problem along these general lines. It is not sufficient, because a Realist may still be an Elementarist with respect to relations in general, or to the relations involved in causal and nomic necessitation in particular. But a solution in terms of second-order relations is barred to the Nominalist. He must give a Humean account of cause and law, or else embrace the eccentricities of a Singularist account of causation. Lacking universals, a Nominalist cannot relate them! So he is nailed to the Humean or the Singularist cross.

But if both a Humean and a Singularist view of cause and law is unsatisfactory, as is widely recognized, and if the account of cause/law in terms of second-order relations can be made reasonably plausible, then cause and law just by themselves constitute a powerful argument for Realism about universals. I take this to be at least part of what lies behind Peirce's insistence on the link between Realism about universals and the lawfulness of the behaviour of things. Since there is law, Peirce argues, there must be universals.

Let us now try to work out a doctrine of necessitation more fully. The first point which an Empiricist must insist upon is that the relation between universals involved is not *logical* necessitation. (Cook Wilson, whose view was otherwise similar to ours, held that the relation was logical. See the last section of this chapter.)

In ch. 17 it was argued that different predicates which are both open and pure may apply to the very same class of particulars, and apply in virtue of the very same universals or range of universals, but apply in semantically different ways. "Naming" predicates simply tag the universal(s) in question, "analysing" predicates elucidate, in some degree at least, the complex nature of the universal(s). (If the universals are not complex, then no analysing predicate applies.) "External" predicates, such as 'brittle', identify a universal or range of universals by reference to relations which the particulars falling under the predicate have to other particulars of a further sort.

Now where there is nomic necessitation it is possible, by suitable choice of *external* predicates, to present the connection as a logical one. It is in this trivial fashion that parents logically necessitate the production of their children. But if naming or analysing predicates are used exclusively, there will not even appear to be logical links between nomically linked universals. Such higher-order but non-logical relations have to be discovered empirically, by the methods of natural science, in particular by the experimental method. Where any such relation holds, it is logically possible that it should not have held. This last is another insight preserved by Humean analyses.

The great difficulty which anybody of an Empiricist temper must feel about these second-order relations is that they are too good to be true. They appear to solve the problem of the nature of nomic causation in a purely verbal way. Tooley tries to get over the apparent difficulty by explicitly making the second-order relations theoretical or postulational. They are those relations between universals which account for the constant conjunction of particulars falling under universals.

But I think it is also useful to consider the parallel case of properties of first-order universals. Suppose that P has the property of *being complex*. It was argued in ch. 23 § 1 that this is a genuine second-order property, not analysable in terms of properties of first-order particulars. If P is complex, then, it is clear, the particulars which are P (by the Principle of Instantiation there are such particulars) must themselves be complex in nature. This is the "descent to first-order particulars". There are Ps and for all $x$, if $x$ is P, then $x$ is complex in nature. Yet this entailed proposition does not entail that P is complex. P might be simple, yet every $x$ that is P be complex in nature because it had other properties besides P.

Similarly, suppose that P (*being P*) nomically necessitates Q (*being Q*). P is instantiated, by the Principle of Instantiation. There are Ps, and, for all $x$, if $x$ is P, then $x$ is Q. This is the "descent to first-order particulars". (Actually, we shall have to qualify this proposition in one, currently irrelevant, respect.) Yet this entailed proposition ("the Humean proposition") does not entail that P nomically necessitates Q. If we admit the phenomenon in the case of second-order properties, why not also in the case of second-order relations?

Humeans, of course, try to reduce cause and law to nothing but constant conjunction. But even they see that this reduction is counter-intuitive. Intuitively, it is all too easy to draw the distinction between genuine law and mere coincidence, even coincidence at the cosmic level. This intuition is respected by our analysis. Although nomic necessity entails constant conjunction, constant conjunction does not entail nomic necessity. Constant conjunction is a mere indication that nomic necessity is present. It is the function of the experimental method to sort out genuine nomic connection from mere coincidence. If the coincidence were genuinely cosmic, then, of course, experimental method would unhappily fail to detect it.

Let us pass now from the topic of nomic connection generally to causal connection in particular. *Being Q* necessitating *being R* is not, of course, in general a case of causation. Causation is a complex affair. It can, however, be brought under this formula as a special case. Let us suppose that a certain object, $a$, is acted upon and, as a result, during the succeeding interval, t, it undergoes a series of changes, E. The predicate 'undergoes E during interval t' applies to object $a$ now. What is more, since E is a perfectly definite sequence of properties, and t is, let us suppose, a perfectly determinate lapse of time – five seconds exactly, for instance – *undergoes E during a lapse of time t* will be a true property. We may think of it either as a relational property of the particular $a$ *now*, or else as a non-relational structural property of a temporal "slice" of $a$ conceived of as a four-dimensional object. It is this first-order property which is the second term in the non-symmetrical higher-order relation of nomic necessitation: the relation which determines the nature of the causal sequence. *a's undergoing E during a lapse of time t* is the *thing necessitated* (a certain state of affairs).

So much for the second term of the higher-order relation. What is its first term? This will be given in part by some of the non-relational properties of $a$ at the instant when t begins to elapse: those non-relational properties of $a$ which are relevant to the occurrence

of sequence E in *a* during lapse of time t. What a thing is is relevant
in determining what happens to it. It will also be given by some of
the relational properties of *a* at the same instant. What a thing's
environment is is relevant in determining what happens to it. These
relevant non-relational and relational properties of *a* may be taken
conjunctively. As such, they form a single, very complex, current
property of *a*. Let us call this property "C". It is *being C* which
necessitates *undergoing sequence E during lapse of time t*. A thing of a
certain sort in a certain sort of environment undergoes certain
changes. If there is another particular, *b*, which is also C, it too will
undergo a sequence of the same type. (This is the "descent to first-
order particulars".) A certain sort of state of affairs brings about a
certain sort of state of affairs.

Let us try to flesh this out by analysing an actual case. A sleeve
brushes against a cup on the table. As a result, the cup falls off the
table and smashes. We notice, of course, that the *description* of the
incident just given by no means proceeds in terms of the properties
and relations of the cup and the other objects involved. Still less
does it confine itself to the causally relevant properties and relations
of the objects. This is no embarrassment to a philosophy which
makes a clear-cut distinction between predicates, on the one hand,
and the universals in virtue of which the predicates apply, on the
other. The cup and the other objects will have an indefinite, perhaps infinite, number of properties, non-relational and relational.
But these properties will have to be scientifically determined, to the
extent that they can be determined. A sub-set of the properties are
nomically relevant to, and taken all together necessitate, the exact
result which is produced. "Constant conjunction" is only entailed
at the level of these nomically relevant properties. A sophisticated
Humean, of course, if he accepted objective and universal properties
and relations, could agree with all this.

In ordinary discourse we would probably speak of the contact
with the brushing sleeve as *the* cause of the cup's falling and break-
ing. We would have some warrant for so speaking, and not merely
a practical warrant. For the brushing by the sleeve is the *alteration*
in the situation without which the effect, or some closely similar
effect, would not have occurred. The other factors in the situation
are mere "standing conditions" or, where they are alterations, the
alterations affect the nature of the final outcome only to a small
degree. Nevertheless, all the standing conditions and all the altera-

tions are causally relevant to the final outcome. We must therefore form the notion of the *total cause*. This is a state of affairs: the sleeve, cup and table's having *all* those properties, non-relational and relational, which are causally relevant to the exact outcome. For instance, among the relational properties involved will be ones determined by non-relational properties of the earth and sun together with relations of the earth and sun to the sleeve, cup and table.

At this point, however, we have to face the difficulty, raised for instance by Russell (1926, p. 229), that if we think in terms of total cause, then it will be impossible to stop short of the whole state of the universe at the moment that the sleeve contacts the cup. The reasoning behind the objection is this. The initial state of affairs necessitates the outcome provided only that no external factor interferes. Suppose, for instance, that I was in a position to prevent the fall of the cup but failed to do so because of slow reflexes. It may then seem necessary to include the condition of my reflexes in the total cause. But I too might have been acted upon. Something might have occurred, perhaps even after the brushing of the sleeve, to liven me up so that I still acted in time. Hence the absence of such enlivening factors must also be included. It is then suggested that when we consider all such potential interferences, interference with interference, etc., the resulting regresses cannot stop short of the whole state of the universe at that time. Only then do we reach the *total* cause.

To reason in this way, however, is to panic unnecessarily. The total cause must be complex, but it will not be as complex as that. For it is in fact perfectly compatible with the notion of nomic necessitation that a cause of a complex sort should necessitate an effect (sequence E over time-interval t) *provided nothing interferes*. The qualifying clause arouses an immediate suspicion of circularity, but the suspicion is unfounded. It is compatible with the iron rule of nomic necessity.

As was presaged a few pages earlier, the qualifying clause involves a small weakening of the force of the phrase "constant conjunction" when it is said that nomic necessitation entails constant conjunction. But that is all. The absence of circularity becomes evident when it is remembered that we have rejected negative universals (ch. 14 § 11). The lack in a particular of a genuine property or relation is not itself a property or relation. Hence to say that particulars with certain properties and in certain relations *plus* an absence of further inter-fering factors nomically necessitate a certain effect would be quite wrong. The absence is *not* a further causal factor. It is true that, given genuine interfering factors (further particulars having certain properties), the original result may be modified or not occur at all. But this is only because, if this addition is made, the total cause will be different. Naturally, it will then necessitate an effect of a different nature.

It is conceivable, indeed, that there is no theoretical upper limit to the additional factors which may be added to the total cause, each extra addition modifying the effect necessitated by the previous total cause. Yet each actual total cause will nomically necessitate its effect.

Distressing as it is for an atheist such as myself to have to admit it, we have here a model for God's interference, by way of miracle, with the working out of ordinary natural processes. It is tempting to argue that, if God can overrule physical necessitations, then they are not really *necessitations* after all. But a physical necessitation does not cease to be a necessitation just because the effect will fail to occur if God interferes. God's inaction in ordinary circumstances is not an extra causal factor in the situation: the physical cause is then the *total* cause. But if God does interfere, then the determinations of his will become part of a new total cause necessitating a different effect.

At this point we may leave the particular question of causality and return to a matter raised by Michael Tooley's argument. Tooley's case seemed to be a powerful argument for saying that laws of nature involve relations between first-order universals. For, in the case of the particles of type A and J which never interact, there seemed no other truth-maker for the law of their interaction. On the other hand, however, if the form of a law of nature is that *being F* necessitates *being G*, and if we accept the Principle of Instantiation (Tooley, it may be noted, is inclined not to), there is in this case no property of *being F*. Being *F*, in this case, would be a matter of an A-type par-ticle having a relation of the sort R to a J-type particle. But, by hypothesis, this never occurs. So the case seems to threaten the par-ticular view of nomic necessity which I (as opposed to Tooley) have adopted. *A fortiori*, it may be noted, there could be no "descent to first-order particulars" in such cases.

I suggest that Tooley's "law" is not really a law, but is simply a *potential* law. A potential law I conceive of as more than a merely logically possible law. It is a "real potential". What, then, is the truth-maker for such a potential law? Will not a second-order relation still be required between the first-order universals, *being an A-type particle*, *R*, and *being a J-type particle*? If so, calling it a "potential" law is no more than a verbal soother.

I suggest, however, that the truth-maker for such a potential law would be simply the three universals themselves. Consider the case of an actual law. Although the universals involved do not logically necessitate the relation, nevertheless the relation of nomic necessitation holds in virtue of the universals being what they are. (It is part of the *nature* of *being F* to necessitate *being G*.) So, my suggestion is, in the case of a merely potential law, the universals involved are such that *if* the antecedent conditions were to be instantiated, the universals involved would necessitate a certain (in this case unknown) consequent.

I conclude that we can both use Tooley's case to argue for a second-order account of nomic necessity *and* give an analysis of the case which respects the Principle of Instantiation.

## II *Other second-order relations?*

It is to be noted that the relation of nomic necessitation, like the second-order properties admitted in the previous chapter, is a formal or topic-neutral universal. I believe that the thesis of Formalism holds for second-order universals, both monadic and polyadic. An argument against "material" second-order *relations* can, I think, be constructed along the same lines as that directed against "material" second-order properties. But I excuse myself the task of developing it. Here I simply ask what further topic-neutral second-order relations should be admitted.

First-order universals may, of course, be related, without these relations being of the second order. This happens where we can give an analysis of the relation in purely first-order terms. Two properties, P and Q, may be *conjuncts of the same conjunctive property*. This appears to be a genuine polyadic universal. But for this relation to hold it is logically necessary and sufficient that there be a first-order particular, *x*, such that *x* is P and *x* is Q. This first-order state of affairs *constitutes* the relation. By contrast, our present interest is in the question whether there are other, *irreducible*, second-order relations besides nomic necessitation.

I suggest that there are only two further such candidates: *nomic exclusion* and *nomic probabilification*.

Nomic exclusion will have as its general form: *being F* nomically excludes *being G* (where F and G may be relations as well as properties). It would have to be added that although, by hypothesis, the particulars which are F are never G, nevertheless there are (existing at some time) particulars which are G. Otherwise the Principle of Instantiation would fail for G, G would not then be a genuine universal, and there would be nothing for F to have a second-order relation to. It will, of course, be an empirical question whether there is an actual relation of nomic exclusion holding between universals. (Tom Richards suggests that Pauli's Exclusion Principle may be an example.) Equally, it is an empirical question whether there is a relation of nomic necessitation.

Between nomic necessitation and nomic exclusion falls nomic probabilification. Indeed, nomic necessitation may be thought of as the highest degree of probabilification (degree 1), and nomic exclusion as the lowest (degree 0). The notion of probabilification is somewhat difficult, but I believe that it can be admitted. The suggestion is that *being F*, say, should probabilify *being G*, without necessitating it or excluding it. Presumably the "descent to first-order particulars" must occur. In order to satisfy this demand it seems that a proportion of the (timeless) class of Fs must be Gs, a proportion answering to the degree of probabilification. The notion of proportions of infinite classes leads to difficulties, and the class of Fs may be an infinite class. But perhaps that problem can be overcome. Orthodox transfinite arithmetic notwithstanding, there does seem to be *some* clear sense in which the class of the even natural numbers is half the size of the class of the natural numbers.

In order to get a genuinely probabilifying relation, it will have to be stipulated that there is no universal, U, such that *being F and being U* necessitates *being G*, while *being F*, yet not being U, excludes *being G*. (Or, alternatively, no U such that *being F and being U* excludes *being G*, while *being F*, yet not being U, necessitates *being G*.)

Such higher-order "relations of partial necessitation", which at the level of first-order particulars incline but do not necessitate absolutely, seem to be a possibility. If so, second-order relations could be invoked even in the case of probabilistic laws. If all laws are probabilistic, then they will be the only sort of second-order relation.

Even if there are relations of full necessitation between particular universals, this does not entail the truth of strict determinism. For there might be other relations between universals which were probabilifying only. At the same time, we did notice in ch. 16 § 1, that unless a property or relation bestows a power, active or passive, upon its particulars, there is no reason to postulate its existence. Furthermore, it is only to the extent that different universals bestow (generically) different powers upon particulars that they can be identified as different universals. By giving an explanation of causal necessity, and nomic necessity generally, in terms of second-order relations we have, in effect, linked power with second-order relations. So we can now rephrase the doctrine of ch. 16 by saying that it is only to the extent that universals enter into relations with each other that they can be known. This gives a pragmatic justification for the principle that *every* universal enters into such relations with at least one other universal, and that, directly or *via* other universals, every universal is linked with every other universal. This is still not a justification of strict determinism because in particular cases, or in all cases, the relation may only be one of nomic probabilification. But it does show that "the realm of universals" (to speak in illegitimately Platonic language) must be a unified realm, so far as it can be known.

Before ending this section we should take brief note of cases where, *prima facie*, a first-order particular is related to a universal, or set of universals. Pink may be Angela's favourite colour. Angela, a first-order particular, appears to stand in relations to the set of the determinate shades of pink, which are first-order universals. When investigated, however, such cases seem to involve causal or at least nomic connection. Crudely, things which are pink have a certain sort of effect upon Angela. *Things* with the 'pink' properties have an effect of a certain nature (roughly indicated) upon Angela. Her special properties are unspecified, but she must have certain properties which predispose her to this effect. What is really involved, then, is a relation between first-order universals.

### III *Do second-order relations fall under universals?*

It was noted in § 1 that in causal situations the universals between which relations of necessitation (or probabilification) hold are extremely complex. When it is also remembered that, according to the argument of this book, there are no determinable but only *determinate* universals – no length, only determinate length, no mass, only determinate mass – it will be seen that the "constant conjunction" involved in causal necessitation is a fairly theoretical affair. If that cause is repeated, then the same effect follows. But in macroscopic causal transactions, at any rate, there is no special reason to think that just that cause will ever be repeated.

However, this is not the end of the matter. It was pointed out in ch. 22 § v that laws of nature are not generally of the simple form 'for all $x$, if $x$ is P, then $x$ is Q', where P and Q are properties. Instead we find a functional correlation, a concomitant variation, between classes of universals. Very often, at least, these classes will be classes of determinate universals all 'falling under the same determinable', for instance the class of all the different temperatures which are actually instantiated. We have discussed the principle of unity of such classes: it is a matter of partial identities linking the individual universals one to another.

The cause, then, will have among its properties one member of the class K, where K is a certain structured class of determinate properties. This property is the causally relevant property of the cause, that property in virtue of which the particular which is the cause brings about a certain effect. The causally relevant property of the effect will be a member of a similar structure class L. The relation of nomic necessitation (or probabilification) will be given by a function which links individual members of K with individual members of L. The function picks out a relation between universals. Where the causally relevant properties of the cause and the effect are complex, as they will be in macroscopic contexts at least, the function will be a resultant of simpler functions. It is the *latter* which we think of as "the laws of nature".

At this point we are ready to raise the question whether there are any third-order universals under which the second-order relations of necessitation, probabilification and exclusion fall. I cannot see what third-order *relations* such relations might have to each other, but perhaps they could have certain *properties*. In the previous chapter we denied that second-order properties could have properties, but the case may be different for second-order relations.

Let us first ask the following question. Suppose it is a fact of nature (as it often seems to be) that for a certain class of causal sequences (or other nomic connections) an identical function conducts us from a particular member of class K to the appropriate member of class L. Do we not then have exactly the same sort of nomic necessity in each case? Will not this identity be a (formal) property of the second-order relations involved? And, if so, will not the identity be a third-order property?

At this point, however, we must pause. We are taking it that *nomic necessitation* (to use this as our example) is a second-order relation, and therefore a genuine universal. If there are to be properties of this relation, then they, the properties, must be reflected in every pair of instances falling under the relation. Only so will there be a full "descent to the particulars" (in this case descent to second-order universals). The third-order property cannot simply be a formal property possessed by *nomic necessitation* when it connects the members of the particular classes of universals, K and L. Such a restricted "property" of nomic necessitation, if it obtains, is something to be analysed in second-order terms.

If *nomic necessitation* is to have a property, then, it will have to be something exhibited by every instance of nomic necessity linking pairs of universals. The necessities of nature will have to have a common form. At the same time, of course, the *a posteriori* nature of our Realism demands that the existence of this form be mere fact, not a logical necessity.

The necessities of nature could have a common form, by cosmic accident as it were. This is parallel to a logically possible first-order cosmic accident: a Humean universe without nomic necessity which mimics a world which is subject to that necessity. But, although not logically conclusive, the lawful behaviour of the universe is the best evidence there is for nomic necessities (or probabilifications). Equally, the display of a common pattern to all nomic necessities would be the best, although not logically conclusive, evidence for ascribing a property to the second-order relation of *nomic necessitation*. The same would hold, of course, for *nomic probabilification* to different degrees and also for *exclusion*.

We do not even yet know which of the possible second-order relations hold between first-order universals. There is some suggestion that the laws of nature conform to some general pattern. But the question whether there are in fact properties of the nomic relations seems in the present state of our knowledge a highly speculative question.

The chart which follows tries to give a synoptic view of the positions which we have adopted concerning higher-order universals. Concerning third-order universals, the only possible types which we have not discussed even briefly are relations of second-order properties (*viz.* relations of properties of first-order properties and relations of properties of first-order relations). I will only say here that I see no reason to think that such universals are possible. Nor do I see any reason to think that fourth-order universals are possible.

## IV *Epistemological problems*

There are no especial problems involved in coming to know that a first-order particular has a certain property, or that two or more particulars are related in a certain way. The simplest case is that of perception. A particular with property, P, acts upon our sense-organs, acting in virtue of being P, and, as a result, we apply a certain concept to the particular. This concept is, perhaps, the concept of a certain disjunctive range of properties, but it is a range of which P is a member. There is no difficulty in principle in the indefinite narrowing of the range (see ch. 22 § IV).

But it may be thought that there are difficulties in coming to know that universals fall under higher-order universals. In particular, how can we come to know nomic necessities? We are pretty well committed to saying that we have such knowledge. The situation mentioned in the previous paragraph is itself a case in point. We can surely *know*, if we can know anything, that a particular has acted upon our sense-organs in a certain way. But action is causality, and causality, we have argued, involves nomic necessity which involves a relation of necessitation between universals. How is knowledge of such necessitation possible?

The obvious first answer is: by use of the methods of science. In particular, we use the experimental method to determine what causes what, and what (nomically) necessitates what. The position of Cook Wilson is of interest here. He takes the experimental method to be a way of *sorting out* necessary connections from mere conjunctions:

> the Eliminative method only disentangles out of a mass of mere conjunctions those which are necessary, finds, that is, which member of the complex belongs to which other in consequence of their own nature. (1926, p. 596)

| FIRST-ORDER PARTICULARS | FIRST-ORDER UNIVERSALS (SECOND-ORDER PARTICULARS) | SECOND-ORDER UNIVERSALS (THIRD-ORDER PARTICULARS) | THIRD-ORDER UNIVERSALS |
|---|---|---|---|
| PARTICULARS | PROPERTIES / RELATIONS | PROPERTIES (1) / RELATIONS (2) / PROPERTIES (1) / RELATIONS (2) | ~~PROPERTIES~~ (3) / ~~RELATIONS~~ (5) / PROPERTIES (4) / ~~RELATIONS~~ (5) / ~~PROPERTIES~~ (3) / ~~RELATIONS~~ (5) / PROPERTIES (4) / ~~RELATIONS~~ (5) |

*Nominalism:* Asserts that there is nothing to the right of the dotted line

* *Elementarism:* Asserts that there is nothing to the right of the heavy line.

*Formalism:* Asserts that everything to the right of the heavy line is a formal or topic-neutral universal

(1) It is argued in ch. 23 § I that these exist, but are all formal
(2) It is argued in ch. 24 §§ I & II that these exist, but are all nomic connections of a formal sort
(3) It is argued in ch. 23 § II that these do not exist
(4) It is suggested in ch. 24 § III that these may exist
(5) It is briefly suggested in ch. 24 § III that we should not postulate these

I accept this view, but it only raises a further problem. All that experiments and observations can do, it would seem, is to determine what invariably goes with what. Relations of necessitation between universals, although they ensure such invariability (with qualifications already noted), are not exhausted by that invariability. Must we then say that the higher-order relation is a mere theoretical postulation, never observed directly but simply posited in order to explain the actually observed regularities? Such a postulation may be satisfactory but is, for my taste, a little too like the postulations of "abstract" classes, possible worlds and the like, which we rejected in ch. 12.

This difficulty did not arise for Cook Wilson. He holds that we do observe necessitation between universals: in the realm of mathematics, in particular. For him, the distinction between logical and nomic necessity is a purely epistemological one. He writes:

> In mathematics we *understand* the necessity of the connexion . . . But there are other kinds of necessary connexion where our knowledge of one element does not show the necessary connexion of it with another, and where we have recourse to experiment and observation; and our knowledge about the connexion has to be . . . a mediated inference. (1926, p. 593)

If, however, we distinguish logical and nomic necessity, as I hold that we should, then this treatment of the problem is unavailable. Must we then take nomic necessity to be a purely theoretical notion?

I suggest, however, that Cook Wilson errs in taking the experimental method to be the only way there is of acquiring knowledge of nomic necessity. I believe that we have *direct*, that is, non-inferential, knowledge of nomic connection. This knowledge, although non-inferential, must not be thought to be logically indubitable. Non-inferential belief in nomic connection may be refined, modified or abandoned in the light of the indirect evidence afforded by experiment and scientific argument generally. But, I assert, there is direct awareness of nomic necessitation. Indeed, the cases I have in mind are familiar ones. I refer to the direct *perceptual* awareness which we appear to have of the operation of causes.

The Louvain psychologist, A. Michotte, argued that there is direct *visual* awareness of causal sequences (1963). His own experiments presuppose that such awareness is sometimes illusory awareness. But he established a strong case for saying that there is a direct, if sometimes fallible, visual perception of certain sorts of causal sequence. It must be admitted, however, that his results concerning vision admit of different interpretations. As Michotte himself points out, cases of a much more knock-down sort are provided by *tactual* perception, in particular the perception of pressure on our body. It is analytic that if something presses, it acts causally. So if we are directly aware of pressure, as we often seem to be, then we are directly aware of causation. But the concept of causation, we have argued, involves nomic necessity (or probabilification) which, we have argued further, is a relation between universals.

However, even the case of the perception of pressure is not absolutely knock-down. It can be argued that when we are aware of pressure on our body, the immediate or non-inferential object of awareness is simply a pressure-*sensation*. This sensation in itself involves no awareness of causality. But we learn to infer that, when we have sensations of this sort, then, normally at least, some physical thing is pressing upon a certain part of our body with a certain force.

I think that this "inferential" view of bodily pressure-perception faces great difficulties. First, a sensation of physical pressure appears to involve essentially the notion of physical pressure. Physical pressure is the intentional object of such sensation. It seems impossible, as a matter of phenomenology, to extract a content from pressure-sensations which can be separated from, and externally correlated with, physical pressure. Second, there is the problem, given this correlational view, of how sensations of pressure are ever connected with physical pressures of varying intensities acting on varying parts of the body. Is this done by the observing of correlations? If so, what sense is employed for the task? It would be ironical if the answer given is vision! Would that imply that there was non-inferential visual perception of causality? If not, how could visual observations assist in building up the correlations?

If we think biologically, we shall at once see the overwhelming importance to any animal of the perception of pressure upon its body. It seems most likely that this perception is non-inferential.

Let it be granted, then, that in tactual perception, if nowhere else, we are directly aware of causal relationships (between particulars). Our concept of causality, I have argued, involves the concept of law-like connection which involves the concept of nomic necessity which involves the concept of a relation between universals.

It is true, of course, that to be aware of a causal sequence, and to be aware that it is causal, does not entail that we are aware of the *properties* of the cause and the effect which make it a causal sequence. In terms of our theory of nomic necessitation, our awareness that a certain sequence is causal, although involving an implicit awareness of a higher-order relation of nomic necessitation, does not involve any more than the roughest awareness of the nature of the terms of that relation. But this does not matter. The establishing of the nature of the terms can be left to the more delicate instrument which is the experimental method. All that was required to be shown is that there is a direct (non-inferential) knowledge of instances falling under the higher-order relation of nomic necessitation. The fact that this non-inferential knowledge is, at least in the state of nature, confined to the knowledge that such a relation holds, without anything but the sketchiest non-inferential knowledge of the nature of the terms between which it holds, does not matter.

There still remains a question in philosophical psychology. What is it for a person to know non-inferentially that a certain particular situation involves a (not fully specified) higher-order relation? I have discussed this question in an earlier book (Armstrong, 1973, in particular ch. 13 § iv). Encouragingly, it turns out that such indeterminate knowledge, knowledge of a mere existentially quantified proposition, is in fact easier to give an account of than knowledge of specified universal connections.

I should be the first to concede that in this chapter we have been seeing, as through a glass, darkly. But we seem to have seen something very exciting. We seem to have seen the possibility that a theory of objective universals may rescue us from Humean scepticism about the reality of causal and nomic connection. In this way, we secure the logical foundations of the scientific enterprise. At the same time, our Realism remains an *a posteriori* Realism. There are, as Hume would put it, no (logically) necessary connections between distinct existences. Experience must inform us, not only what first-order particulars there are and what their nature is, but also how they are nomically connected.

# *In conclusion*

In the *Parmenides* young Socrates, after declaring his faith in the theory of Forms, is asked by Parmenides what he takes the *extent* of the realm of the Forms to be (130 a–d). That question has confronted not merely Platonists, but every Realist about universals, ever since. My suggestion has been that the Empiricist, at least, should answer that for the most part it is not up to the philosopher to answer the question. There is much that he can say about the nature of the question and the *form* that answers should take. This work, long as it is, has only begun to grapple with the problems involved. But the *content* of the answer must be determined, not by abstract reasoning, but by the natural sciences with their ultimate dependence upon observation and experiment.

However, as the discussion has developed, what has been presented is not simply a theory of universals but a first philosophy or ontology, a theory of the nature of reality in its most general aspect. Not every topic which a first philosophy might be expected to cover has been covered, but comprehensiveness may be too much to expect. Perhaps it should not even be sought.

At any rate, if what has been offered is a first philosophy, it may be appropriate to conclude by considering where the main difficulty for this philosophy appears to lie. I think that the answer to this question is clear. It is the difficulty which faces any Empiricist philosophy: the problem of necessary truth. Can an Empiricist give a satisfactory account of the logically necessary truths of mathematics, of logic, of philosophy itself, especially first philosophy?

The problem disappears if there are no necessary truths, if the whole distinction between logically necessary and contingent truths is not a real one. This is the view of Quine, denier of distinctions. But I find this extreme Empiricist view difficult to accept. The "Rational sciences" of logic and mathematics can be, and are, developed in a purely *a priori* manner. This would not be possible if their propositions had no different logical status from those of the natural sciences.

It is clear, then, that what is required is an Empiricist theory of necessary truth. If an Empiricist theory of necessary truth can be developed at all, it is clear what general form it must take. The source of necessity must be located in the words, or concepts, in which the propositions are expressed. What the details of this theory are to be, and how various powerful objections to such a theory are to be overcome, I do not know. One objection, however, which I cannot take seriously is the contention that the notions of meaning, and hence synonymy, are irremediably confused.

But what of the theory of universals put forward in this book? A great deal of our argument has consisted in the rejection of alleged *a priori* necessities. It has been pointed out that there are logical possibilities open where earlier theories saw only contradiction. An example is the rejection in this book of the necessity for simple universals. Logical Atomism proclaims their necessity. But we have argued that logic cannot determine the matter.

Nevertheless, at a few points our arguments seemed to bind rather than to loose. A conspicuous example is the link between particularity and universality. It was argued that every particular must have properties and relations (though no particular properties and relations). Equally it was argued that every property and relation must be a property and relation of some particular (though not of any particular particular).

The connection between particularity and universality is so close that we can do no more than draw Scotus' 'formal distinction' between them. Here we seem to be in the presence of a logical necessity in things. Yet we are committed to the denial of any *de re* logical necessity. Can we find some account of this distinction, and of our knowledge of it, which is compatible with Empiricism?

# Glossary of terms used and principles formulated

(Principles and notions rejected are *starred*.
Principles and notions introduced in volume 1 are prefaced by "1".)

1 *Abstract particulars*. Particulars of which there can be more than one at the same place and time; also (*) properties and relations as particulars (Stout).

*Anomoeomerous property*. A property is anomoeomerous if and only if it is not homoeomerous (*q.v.*).

1 *A posteriori Realism*. The doctrine that what universals there are has to be established *a posteriori*, on the basis of total science.

1 *A priori Realism*. The doctrine that what universals there are can be established *a priori*, for instance on the basis of meanings.

1 *Argument from Meaning*. Argument to universals from the meanings of predicates.

1 *Aristotelian Realism*. Immanent Realism (*q.v.*).

1 *Bare particulars*. Particulars which lack properties, or which lack both properties and relations (see Bare particulars, rejection of, the Weak and Strong Principles).

1 *Bare particulars, rejection of, the Strong Principle*. For each particular, *x*, there exists at least one non-relational property, P, such that *x* is P.

1 *Bare particulars, rejection of, the Weak Principle*. For each particular, *x*, there exists at least one universal, U, such that *x* is U.

1 *Bit theory*. See Mereological Nominalism.

1 *Bundle theory of particulars*. The doctrine that a particular is nothing but a "bundle" of properties conceived of as universals (see Universalism).

1 *Cases*. Properties and relations as particulars (Wolterstorff).

1 *Class Nominalism*. The reductive doctrine that for particulars to have the same property, or to have the same relation, is for them to be members of the same class of particulars.

*Closed predicate.* A predicate such that its semantics restrict its application to a finite number of particulars.

1 *\*Complete complex of compresence.* A class of (universal) properties such that each member of the class is compresent with each other member of the class, and there is no property compresent with each member of the class which is not a member of the class. Used by Russell as the definition of a particular.

1 *\*Compresence.* Primitive relation holding between any two members of the class of properties which, on a Bundle theory of particulars (*q.v.*), go to make a particular.

1 *\*Concept Nominalism.* The reductive doctrine that for particulars to have the same property, or to have the same relation, is for them to fall under the same concept.

1 *Concrete particulars.* Particulars such that no two can occupy the very same places and times.

*\*Conjunction Principle, the.* If F is a property, and G is a property which is part of that property, then whatever particulars have F also have G.

*Conjunctive universals, Principle of.* If U is a universal, and U' is a distinct universal, and there are particulars which have U and U', then $U\&U'$ is a universal.

*Counter-correspondence.* The semantic relation holding between a sentence 'Pa' and a state of affairs Qa, where $P \neq Q$.

*Descent to first-order particulars.* The principle that for any higher-order property or relation of order N, it is not simply instantiated by universals of order $N - 1$, but is reflected in the particulars falling under these latter universals, and so on down until first-order particulars are reached.

*Disjunctive Universals, rejection of.* If U is a universal, and U' is a distinct universal, it is not the case that $U \lor U'$ is a universal.

*Dissective predicate.* Goodman's term for a homoeomerously applicable predicate.

1 *\*Dissimilarity of the Diverse.* McTaggart's term for the Identity of Indiscernibles (*q.v.*).

1 *\*Distributive unity.* Form of unity postulated by Stout to obtain between all those particularized properties and relations which have the same (universal) property or relation.

*\*Elementarism.* The doctrine that, although there are universals, there are no second- or higher-order universals.

*Emergent property.* An anomoeomerous property (*q.v.*) which is not a structural property (*q.v.*).

*Empty predicates.* Pure predicates (*q.v.*) which lack application or, if they apply, do not apply in virtue of universals.

1 *\*Equality.* Relation said to hold between particularized properties and relations which are of the same kind, e.g. by G. Küng.

*\*Essentialist Realism.* Doctrine that substantival universals (*q.v.*) are not reducible to conjunctions of properties.

*External Relation.* A relation which is not logically determined by the nature of the related terms.

*Family predicates.* Pure, open, predicates (*q.v.*) applying in virtue of a class of universals, where the members of the class are united by resemblance but not by a unitary, topic-neutral, formula.

1 *Formal distinction.* The non-relational distinction which Scotus holds can be drawn between the haecceity (*q.v.*) and the nature of a particular.

*Formalism.* The doctrine that all higher-order universals are formal or topic-neutral in nature.

1 *Haecceity.* Scotist term for the particularity, or thisness, of particulars.

*Heterogeneous predicates.* Pure, open predicates (*q.v.*) applying in virtue of a class of heterogeneous universals.

1 *Higher-order particulars.* Properties and relations considered as having properties and relations.

1 *Higher-order universals.* Properties and relations of properties and relations.

*Homoeomerously applicable predicates.* A predicate such that, if it is applicable to a particular, it is applicable to any part of that particular.

*Homoeomerous property.* A property is homoeomerous if and only if for all particulars, $x$, which have the property, then for all parts $y$ of $x$, $y$ has that property.

*Homogeneous predicates.* Pure, open predicates (*q.v.*) which do not apply in virtue of a single universal, but in virtue of a class of universals united by a unitary, topic-neutral, formula.

1 *\*Identity of Indiscernibles.* The view that different particulars cannot have all the same properties. In the *Strong* form of the doctrine the properties are confined to non-relational properties; in the *Weak* form all properties are included.

1 *Identity view.* The view that properties and relations are universals.

1 *Immanent Realism*. The doctrine which admits universals but denies that they are transcendent.

*Impure predicates*. Predicates which involve essential reference to a particular, e.g. 'descended from Charlemagne'.

1 *Indiscernibility of Identicals*. If *a* and *b* are the very same particular, then any property is a property of *a* if and only if it is a property of *b*.

1 *\*Inherence*. Converse of the relation of *support* (*q.v.*).

*Instantial Invariance, Principle of*. For all *n*, if a universal is *n*-adic with respect to a particular instantiation, then it is *n*-adic with respect to all its instantiations (it is *n*-adic *simpliciter*).

1 *Instantiation, Principle of*. For each *n*-adic universal, U, there exist at least *n* particulars such that they are U.

*\*Intensional Principle*. If predicates are not logically equivalent, and are not logically empty, then they cannot apply, where they do apply, in virtue of the same universal or range of universals.

*Internal Relation*. A relation which is logically determined by the nature of the related terms.

*Internal Relations, the Reductive principle for*. If two or more particulars are internally related, then the relation is nothing more than the possession by the particulars of the properties which necessitate the relation.

*Irish principle, the*. If it can be proved *a priori* that a thing falls under a certain universal, then there is no such universal.

1 *\*Lockean view of particulars*. The view that particulars involve a substratum *related* to the properties of the particular.

*\*Logical Atomism*. The view that whatever is complex (including complex universals) must be composed of simples.

*Logical Equivalence, Principle of*. If predicates are logically equivalent, but not logically empty, then they apply, where they do apply, in virtue of the very same universals.

*Logically empty predicates*. A predicate is logically empty if and only if it logically must apply to any object.

1 *Materialism, Reductive*. The doctrine that the concepts and laws of physics are sufficient to give a complete account of the nature of things.

*"Matters of fact"*. See External Relation.

1 *\*Mereological Nominalism*. The reductive doctrine that for particulars to have the same property, or to have the same relation, is for them to be parts of the same aggregate of particulars.

*Monadic Realism.* The view that all polyadic universals are analysable in terms of monadic universals.

*Monadic Relation.* Term sometimes used by Russell to mean 'property'.

1 *Naturalism.* The hypothesis that nothing but Nature, the single, all-embracing spatio-temporal system, exists.

1 *Nature.* The single, all-embracing spatio-temporal system.

1 *Nature of a particular.* The complete conjunction of a particular's properties, itself a property.

*Negative universals, rejection of.* If U is a universal, then it is not the case that $\sim U$ is a universal.

*Nominal essence.* The collection of those properties of a particular falling under some substantival universal(s) (*q.v.*), which are diagnostic of its being a certain sort of stuff or certain sort of thing.

1 *Nominalism.* The doctrine that whatever exists is a particular, and nothing but a particular.

1 *Non-Identity assumption.* The assumption that a Form cannot participate in itself.

1 *Objectivist theories of properties and relations.* Any doctrine which gives an account of the properties and relations of particulars as existing independently of the relation of the particulars to minds or systems of classification.

1 *Object regress.* Attempts to criticize Relational analyses (*q.v.*) by showing that the entities appealed to by such analyses themselves require the very same analysis.

1 *One over Many argument.* The argument to universals from the apparent existence of identities of nature between different particulars.

*Open predicate.* A predicate such that nothing in its semantics restricts its application to a finite number of particulars.

*(?) Order Invariance, Principle of.* For all N, if a universal has particulars of order N in one instantiation, then it has particulars of the same order in all instantiations.

*Order Invariance, Weak Principle of.* If there are a number of particulars and a relation which relates them, then each particular is a particular of the same order.

1 *Participation.* Relation which it was suggested that particulars have to Forms.

I *Particularism.* The doctrine that the properties and relations of particulars are themselves (first-order) particulars.

*Particularization, Principle of.* The principle that each particular exemplifies at least one monadic universal which is a particularizing universal (*q.v.*), at least weakly.

I *Particularized qualities.* Qualities as particulars (Strawson).

I *Particularizing universals.* Universals which yield an unambiguous answer to the question whether or not a particular is *one* instance of that universal. If the universal "divides its instantiations", yielding nothing but discrete, non-overlapping particulars, then it particularizes *strongly.* If not, it particularizes *weakly.*

I *Perfect particulars.* Properties and relations as particulars (Bergmann).

I *Platonic Realism.* See Transcendent Realism.

I *Predicate Nominalism.* The reductive doctrine that for particulars to have the same property, or have the same relation, is for the same predicate to apply to them.

I *Predicates, identity-conditions for.* Predicate tokens are of identical type if and only if they are synonymous.

*Property abstraction, Principle of.* Defined by Grossmann as ". . . there exists a property *g* which an entity *e* has *if and only if . . . e . . .* where the dots indicate any well-formed propositional context."

I *Property-instances.* Properties as particulars.

*Property-predicates.* Strictly universal predicates (*q.v.*) where the universal in question is a property.

I *Propositional predicate.* The predicate of a proposition (as opposed to a sentence).

*Pure predicate.* A predicate which applies to particulars purely in virtue of the universals which the particulars instantiate.

*Real essence.* The collection of those properties of a particular falling under some substantival universal(s) (*q.v.*) which determine its nominal essence (*q.v.*).

I *Realism.* The doctrine that there are universals.

*Reflexive relations.* If a particular has a relation to itself, then it may be said to be reflexively related. If a relation is such that in all its instantiations it relates a particular to itself, it may be said to be a reflexive relation.

I *Relational analysis.* Any doctrine which gives a reductive account of a particular's having properties or relations in terms of further *relations* between the particular and some further entity or entities.

1 *\*Relational Immanent Realism.* The form of Immanent Realism (*q.v.*) which takes the particularity and universality of particulars to be *related* constituents of the particulars.

*Relational Realism.* The doctrine that there are no *irreducible* monadic universals.

*Relation-predicates.* Strictly universal predicates (*q.v.*) where the universal in question is a relation.

*"Relations of ideas".* See Internal Relation.

1 *Relation regress.* Attempts to criticize Relational analyses (*q.v.*) by showing that the relations appealed to by such analyses themselves require the same analysis.

*Relation rope.* The totality of relations holding between two (or more) particulars (Williams).

*Resemblance of particulars. a* resembles *b* if and only if there exists a property, P, such that *a* has P, and there exists a property, Q, such that *b* has Q, and *either* P = Q *or* P resembles Q.

1 *\*Resemblance Nominalism.* The reductive doctrine that for particulars to have the same property, or have the same relation, is for them to have a sufficient resemblance to some paradigm particular(s).

1 *Restricted Third Man.* A particular case of Plato's Third Man argument (*q.v.*).

1 *Scientific Realism (about universals).* See *A posteriori* Realism.

1 *\*Self-predication assumption.* The view that the Form of F-ness must itself be an F.

1 *\*Singularist theory of causation.* The view that in a causal sequence it is a particular *qua* particular which acts to bring about its effect.

1 *State of affairs.* A particular (including higher-order particulars) having a property, or two or more particulars being related.

1 *\*Stoutian particulars.* Properties and relations as particulars.

*Strictly universal predicates.* A pure predicate (*q.v.*) which applies in virtue of a *single* universal.

*Structural property.* A species of anomoeomerous property (*q.v.*) such that proper parts of particulars having the structural property, S, have property T, which is not identical with S, and such that this state of affairs is, in part at least, constitutive of S. Structural properties are divisible into *relational* and *non-relational* structural properties, depending on whether or not they involve relations.

1 *Subjectivist theories of properties and relations.* Any doctrine which gives an account of the properties and relations of particulars in terms of the relation of the particulars to systems of classification and/or minds.

1 *Substance, Hume's definition of.* Whatever is logically capable of independent existence.

*Substantival universals.* Monadic universals associated with the "whole nature" of kinds of stuff (e.g. gold) or kinds of things (e.g. electrons).

1 *Substrata.* The particularity of particulars conceived of as *related* to the properties and relations of the particulars (see Relational Immanent Realism).

1 *Support.* Relation supposed to obtain between substrata and properties in the Relational form of Immanent Realism (*q.v.*).

1 *Third Bed argument.* Plato's "argument" to show that Forms are essentially unique.

1 *Third Man argument.* Plato's argument to show that the theory of Forms is involved in an infinite regress.

1 *Tie.* The non-relational connection between particularity and universality argued for by the non-relational form of Immanent Realism (*q.v.*).

1 *Total position.* The spatio-temporal area occupied by a particular from the beginning to the end (if any) of its existence.

1 *Transcendent Realism.* The doctrine that universals exist separated from particulars.

1 *Tropes.* Properties and relations as particulars (Williams).

1 *Unit-Properties.* Properties and relations as particulars (Matthews and Cohen).

1 *Universalism.* The doctrine that whatever exists is a universal, and nothing but a universal (see Bundle theory of particulars).

1 *Victory of particularity.* The fact that the "union" of particularity and universality yields a particular, not a universal.

# Works cited
# (in both volumes)

Aaron, R. I. (1939) Two Senses of the Word *Universal, Mind,* 68

Abbot, F. E. (1886) *Scientific Theism,* Macmillan

Anderson, J. (1962) *Studies in Empirical Philosophy,* Angus and Robertson

Anscombe, G. E. M. (1971) Causality and Determination, Inaugural Lecture, Cambridge University Press

Aquinas, St. T. *Summa Theologica,* 3 vols., trans. by the Dominican Fathers, Benziger Brothers 1947–8

Aristotle, *Basic Works,* ed. McKeon, R., Random House 1941

Armstrong, D. M. (1968) *A Materialist Theory of the Mind,* Routledge

Armstrong, D. M. (1973) *Belief, Truth and Knowledge,* Cambridge University Press

Armstrong, D. M. (1974) Infinite Regress Arguments and the Problem of Universals, *Australasian Journal of Philosophy,* 52

Armstrong, D. M. (1975) Towards a Theory of Properties, *Philosophy,* 50

Armstrong, D. M. (1978) Naturalism, Materialism and First Philosophy, *Philosophia,* 8

Ayer, A. J. (1954) *Philosophical Essays,* Macmillan

Ayer, A. J. (1971) *Russell and Moore: The Analytical Heritage,* Macmillan

Barnett, D. (1974) A New Semantical Theory of Egocentric Particulars, *Synthese,* 28

Bergmann, G. (1957) Elementarism, *Philosophy and Phenomenological Research,* 18

Bergmann, G. (1964) *Logic and Reality,* University of Wisconsin Press

Bergmann, G. (1967) *Realism,* University of Wisconsin Press

Berkeley, G. *Principles of Human Knowledge,* in *Berkeley's Philosophical Writings,* ed. Armstrong, D. M., Collier-Macmillan 1965

Berkeley, G. *Three Dialogues between Hylas and Philonous* in *Berkeley's Philosophical Writings,* ed. Armstrong, D. M., Collier-Macmillan 1965

Berry, G. (1968) Logic with Platonism, *Synthese,* 19

Black, M. (1952) The Identity of Indiscernibles, *Mind,* 61, reprinted with additional notes in Black, M., *Problems of Analysis,* Routledge 1954

Black, M. (1971) The Elusiveness of Sets, *The Review of Metaphysics,* 24

Blanshard, B. (1939) *The Nature of Thought,* Allen and Unwin

Blanshard, B. (1962) *Reason and Analysis,* Open Court

Bochenski, I. M. (1956) The Problem of Universals, in *The Problem of Universals,* Notre Dame University Press

Boler, J. F. (1963) *Charles Peirce and Scholastic Realism,* University of Washington Press

Bradley, F. H. (1893a) On Professor James' Doctrine of Simple Resemblance, *Mind*, 2

Bradley, F. H. (1893b) Professor James on Simple Resemblance, *Mind*, 2

Bradley, F. H. (1897) *Appearance and Reality*, 2nd ed., Oxford University Press

Brandt, R. B. (1957) The Languages of Realism and Nominalism, *Philosophy and Phenomenological Research*, 17

Broad, C. D. (1933) *Examination of McTaggart's Philosophy*, vol. 1, Cambridge University Press

Brownstein, D. (1973) *Aspects of the Problem of Universals*, The University of Kansas

Butchvarov, P. (1966) *Resemblance and Identity*, Indiana University Press

Campbell, K. K. (1969) Colours, in *Contemporary Philosophy in Australia*, ed. Brown, R. and Rollins, C. D., Allen and Unwin 1969

Carnap, R. (1967) *The Logical Structure of the World*, trans. George, R. A., Routledge

Chakrabarti, K. (1975) The Nyāya-Vaiśeṣika Theory of Universals, *Journal of Indian Philosophy*, 3

Church, R. W. (1935) *Hume's Theory of the Understanding*, Allen and Unwin

Church, R. W. (1952) *An Analysis of Resemblance*, Allen and Unwin

Clarke, F. P. (1962) St. Thomas on "Universals", *The Journal of Philosophy*, 59

Cook Wilson, J. (1926) *Statement and Inference*, 2 vols., Oxford University Press

Cresswell, M. J. (1975) What is Aristotle's Theory of Universals? *Australasian Journal of Philosophy*, 53

Davidson, D. (1965) Theories of Meaning and Learnable Languages, in *Logic, Methodology and Philosophy of Science*, Proceedings of the 1964 International Congress, ed. Bar-Hillel, Y., North Holland

Demos, R. (1946) A Note on Plato's Theory of Ideas, *Philosophy and Phenomenological Research*, 8

Donagan, A. (1963) Universals and Metaphysical Realism, *The Monist*, 47

Duncan-Jones, A. E. (1934) Universals and Particulars, *Proceedings of the Aristotelian Society*, 34

Durrant, R. G. (1970) Identity of Properties and the definition of 'Good', *Australasian Journal of Philosophy*, 48

Frege, G. (1884) *The Foundations of Arithmetic*, trans. Austin, J. L., Blackwell 1950

Frege, G. (1918–19) The Thought: A Logical Inquiry, trans. A. M. and Marcelle Quinton, *Mind*, 65, 1956, reprinted in *Philosophical Logic*, ed. P. F. Strawson, Oxford University Press 1967

Gallie, W. B. (1952) *Peirce and Pragmatism*, Pelican

Goodman, N. (1956) A World of Individuals, in *The Problem of Universals*, Notre Dame University Press, reprinted with Appendix, in Goodman, N., *Problems and Projects*, Bobbs-Merrill 1972

Goodman, N. (1966) *The Structure of Appearance*, 2nd ed., Bobbs-Merrill

Goodman, N. (1970) Seven Strictures on Similarity, in *Experience and Theory*, ed. Foster, L. and Swanson, J. W., Duckworth, reprinted in Goodman, N., *Problems and Projects*, Bobbs-Merrill 1972

Goodwin, R. P. (1961) Charles Saunders Peirce: A Modern Scotist?, *The New Scholasticism*, 35

Grajewski, M. J. (1944) *The Formal Distinction of Duns Scotus*, The Catholic University of America Press

Grossmann, R. (1972) Russell's Paradox and Complex Properties, *Noûs*, 6

Grossmann, R. (1973) *Ontological Reduction*, Indiana University Press

Grossmann, R. (1974) Meinong's Doctrine of the *Aussersein* of the Pure Object, *Noûs*, 8

Hall, E. W. (1957) Logical Subjects and Physical Objects, *Philosophy and Phenomenological Research*, 17

Hampshire, S. (1950) Scepticism and Meaning, *Philosophy*, 25

Hayek, F. A. (1952) *The Sensory Order*, Routledge

Hendel, C. W. (1963) *Studies in the Philsophy of David Hume*, 2nd ed., Library of Liberal Arts

Hochberg, H. (1965) Universals, Particulars and Predication, *The Review of Metaphysics*, 19

Hochberg, H. (1966) Things and Descriptions, *American Philosophical Quarterly*, 3

Hochberg, H. (1969) Moore and Russell on Particulars, Relations and Identity, in *Studies in the Philosophy of G. E. Moore*, ed. Klemke, E. D., Quadrangle books

Hume, D. *A Treatise of Human Nature*, 2 vols., Everyman (1911)

Husserl, E. (1913) *Logical Investigations*, 2nd ed., trans. Findlay, J. N., Routledge 1970

Jackson, F. C. (1977) Statements about Universals, *Mind*, 86

James, W. (1950) *The Principles of Psychology*, 2 vols., reprinted Dover

Johnson, W. E. (1921) *Logic, Part I*, Cambridge University Press

Johnson, W. E. (1922) *Logic, Part II*, Cambridge University Press

Jones, J. R. (1949) Are the Qualities of Particular Things Universal or Particular?, *Philosophical Review*, 58

Jones, J. R. (1951) Characters and Resemblances, *Philosophical Review*, 60

Jørgenson, J. (1953) Some Reflections on Reflexivity, *Mind*, 62

Jørgenson, J. (1955) On Katsoff's Reflexions on Jørgenson's Reflexions on Reflexivity, *Mind*, 64

Katsoff, L. O. (1955) Some Reflections on Jørgenson's Reflections on Reflexivity, *Mind*, 64

Kearns, J. T. (1968) Sameness or Similarity?, *Philosophy and Phenomenological Research*, 29

Kemp Smith, N. (1927) The Nature of Universals (III), *Mind*, 36

Kretzmann, N. (1970) Medieval Logicians on the Meaning of the *Propositio*, *Journal of Philosophy*, 67

Küng, G. (1964) Concrete and Abstract properties, *Notre Dame Journal of Formal Logic*, 5

Küng, G. (1967) *Ontology and the Logistic Analysis of Language*, revised ed., Reidel

Locke, J. *Essay concerning Human Understanding*, 2 vols., Everyman (1961)

Loux, M. J. (1974) Kinds and the Dilemma of Individuation, *The Review of Metaphysics*, 27

Loux, M. J. (1976) The Concept of a Kind, *Philosophical Studies*, 29

Loux, M. J. Identity and Compresence: An Examination of Russell's later theory of substance, (forthcoming)

Mackie, J. L. (1976) *Problems from Locke*, Oxford University Press

McMullin, E. (1958) The Problem of Universals, *Philosophical Studies*, 8

McTaggart, J. McT. E. (1921) *The Nature of Existence*, 2 vols., Cambridge University Press

Matthews, G. B. and Cohen, S. M. (1968) The One and the Many, *Review of Metaphysics*, 21

Michotte, A. (1963) *The Perception of Causality*, trans. Miles, T. R. and E., Methuen

Mill, J. S., *A System of Logic*, ed. Robson, J. M., University of Toronto Press and Routledge 1973

Moore, G. E. (1953) *Some Main Problems of Philosophy*, Allen and Unwin

O'Connor, D. J. (1946) On Resemblance, *Proceedings of the Aristotelian Society*, 46

Owens, J. (1961) Unity and Essence in St. Thomas Aquinas, *Mediaeval Studies*, 23

Pap, A. (1959) Nominalism, Empiricism and Universals: 1, *Philosophical Quarterly*, 9

Pears, D. (1951) Universals, *Philosophical Quarterly*, 1, reprinted in *Universals and Particulars*, ed. Loux, M. J., Anchor Books 1970

Peirce, C. S., *Collected Papers*, 8 vols., 1931–58, Harvard University Press

Plato, *Parmenides*, trans. Taylor, A. E., Oxford University Press 1934

Plato, *Phaedo*, trans. Gallop, D., Oxford University Press 1975

Plato, *Politicus*, trans. Skemp, J. B. in *Plato's Statesman*, Routledge 1952

Plato, *Republic*, trans. Cornford, F. M., Oxford University Press 1941

Plato, *Sophist*, trans. Cornford, F. M. in *Plato's Theory of Knowledge*, Kegan Paul 1935

Popper K. R. (1973) *Objective Knowledge*, Oxford University Press

Price, H. H. (1953) *Thinking and Experience*, Hutchinson

Prior, A. N. (1949) Determinables, Determinates and Determinants, Part 1, *Mind*, 58

Putnam, H. (1970a) On Properties, in *Essays in Honour of Carl G. Hempel*, ed. Rescher N., Reidel, reprinted in Putnam, H., *Philosophical Papers*, vol. 1, Cambridge University Press 1975

Putnam, H. (1970b) Is Semantics Possible?, in *Language, Belief and Metaphysics*, ed. Kiefer, H. E. and Munitz, M. K., State University of New York Press

Quine, W. V. O. (1960) *Word and Object*, M.I.T. Press

Quine, W. V. O. (1966) *The Ways of Paradox*, Random House

Quine, W. V. O. (1969) *Ontological Relativity*, Columbia University Press

Quinton, A. (1957) Properties and Classes, *Proceedings of the Aristotelian Society*, 48

Quinton, A. (1973) *The Nature of Things*, Routledge

Raphael, D. D. (1955) Universals, Resemblance and Identity, *Proceedings of the Aristotelian Society*, 55

Reid, T. *Essays on the Intellectual Powers of Man*, ed. Woozley, A. D., Macmillan 1941

Russell, B. (1911) On the Relations of Universals and Particulars, *Proceedings of the Aristotelian Society*, 12, reprinted, with an added paragraph, in *Logic and Knowledge*, ed. Marsh, R. C., Allen and Unwin 1956

Russell, B. (1912) *The Problems of Philosophy*, Home University Library

Russell, B. (1918) *The Philosophy of Logical Atomism*, reprinted in *Logic and Knowledge*, ed. Marsh, R. C., Allen and Unwin 1956

Russell, B. (1926) *Our Knowledge of the External World*, Revised ed., Allen and Unwin

Russell, B. (1940) *An Inquiry into Meaning and Truth*, Allen and Unwin

Russell, B. (1948) *Human Knowledge, its Scope and Limits*, Allen and Unwin

Russell, B. (1959) *My Philosophical Development*, Allen and Unwin

Ryle, G. (1939) Plato's Parmenides, *Mind*, 48, reprinted in Ryle, G., *Collected Papers*, vol. I, Hutchinson 1971

Scotus, D. *Opera Omnia*, vol. VIII, Civitas Vaticana 1973

Searle, J. R. (1959) Determinables and the Notion of Resemblance, *Proceedings of the Aristotelian Society*, supp. vol. 33

Searle, J. R. (1969) *Speech Acts*, Cambridge University Press

Shimony, A. (1948) The Status and Nature of Essences, *The Review of Metaphysics*, 1

Smart, J. J. C. (1963) Materialism, *Journal of Philosophy*, 60

Sprigge, T. L. S. (1970) *Facts, Words and Beliefs*, Routledge

Steenburgh, E. W. Van (1974) The Problem of Simple Resemblance, *Philosophical Studies*, 25

Stenius, E. (1974) Sets, *Synthese*, 27

Stout, G. F. (1921) *The Nature of Universals and Propositions*, Oxford University Press (British Academy Lecture), reprinted in Stout, G. F., *Studies in Philosophy and Psychology*, Macmillan 1930

Stout, G. F. (1923) Are the characteristics of particular things universal or particular?, *Proceedings of the Aristotelian Society*, supp. vol. 3

Stout, G. F. (1930) *Studies in Philosophy and Psychology*, Macmillan

Stout, G. F. (1936) Universals again, *Proceedings of the Aristotelian Society*, supp. vol. 15

Strawson, P. F. (1959) *Individuals*, Methuen

Strawson, P. F. (1974) *Subject and Predicate in Logic and Grammar*, Methuen

Thompson, M. H. (1953) On the Distinction between Thing and Property, in *The Return to Reason*, ed. Wild, J., Henry Regnery

Tooley, M. (1977) The Nature of Laws, *Canadian Journal of Philosophy*, 7

Weinberg, S. (1974) Unified Theories of Elementary-Particle Interaction, *Scientific American*, 231

Williams, D. C. (1953) The Elements of Being, *The Review of Metaphysics*, 6, reprinted in Williams, D. C., *Principles of Empirical Realism*, Charles Thomas 1966

Williams, D C. (1963) Necessary Facts, *The Review of Metaphysics*, 16

Williams, D. C. (1966) *Principles of Empirical Realism*, Charles Thomas
Wittgenstein, L. (1922) *Tractatus Logico-Philosophicus*, trans. Pears, D. F. and McGuiness, B. F., Routledge 1961
Wolter, A. B. (1962) The Realism of Scotus, *Journal of Philosophy*, 59
Wolterstorff, N. (1970) *On Universals*, Chicago University Press

# Index to Volumes I and II

For EU product safety concerns, contact us at Calle de José Abascal, 56–1°, 28003 Madrid, Spain or eugpsr@cambridge.org.

www.ingramcontent.com/pod-product-compliance
Ingram Content Group UK Ltd.
Pitfield, Milton Keynes, MK11 3LW, UK
UKHW012344130625
459647UK00009B/525